THE GREAT
MAGNESS
TRIAL

THE GREAT MAGNESS TRIAL

*The Killing of Patton Anderson,
the Trial of the Magness Family,
& the Pursuit of Justice on the
Tennessee Frontier*

JACK MACGREGOR CAMPBELL

BRAYBREE
Publishing

Copyright © 2017 Jack MacGregor Campbell
All rights reserved

Published by BrayBree Publishing Company LLC
FIRST EDITION

No part of this book may be reproduced, stored in or introduced into a retrieval system or transmitted in any form or by any means (electronic, mechanical, photocopying, recording, or otherwise) without the prior written permission of the publisher and copyright owner.

The scanning, uploading, and distribution of this book on the Internet or through any other means is not permitted without permission from the publisher and copyright owner.

ISBN-13: 978-1-940127-12-5

Printed in the United States of America

BrayBree Publishing Company LLC
P.O. Box 1204
Dickson, Tennessee 37056-1204

Visit our website at www.braybreepublishing.com

Front cover images: Shutterstock.com, Library of Congress
Back cover images: Library of Congress, *Nashville Clarion*

For my mother,
Martha Magness (Farris) Campbell

Acknowledgements

In preparing this document, I have compared the histories to the original sources available to me and tried to establish the proper record. A great deal of credit must go to those who originally chronicled the people and trials in the scope of this document without the availability of the complete record. Without their original research, which I have cited throughout the document, it would have been difficult to know where to begin to find original records.

I extend thanks to Pat Bishop, who helped transcribe many of those original handwritten records. For the biographical aspects of this document, I have tried to use original sources to the best of my ability. I have been fortunate to have the extensive and well-documented research of Jeanette Magness Stubblefield, Robert Craig, Verna Magness, and Thomas G. Webb as resources. I also greatly appreciate the assistance of the staff of the Library of Congress, office of the U.S. Senate Historian, the staff of the U.S. Senate Library, the staff of the Tennessee State Library and Archives, and the staff of the Williamson County Tennessee Archives.

Jack MacGregor Campbell

Contents

Foreword *by Donald A. Ritchie* — ix

1. The Killing of Patton Anderson — 3
2. Lawyers of Great Promise — 15
3. The Magness Family — 41
4. Tennessee v. David Magness: The First Trial Begins — 48
5. The Great Lawyers Battle for the Jury — 67
6. Awaiting Justice in Jail: Perrygreen and Jonathan Magness — 101
7. Aftermath of the Trial — 111

Bibliography — 121
Index — 127

Foreword

Lawyers are as intimately linked to politics as love to marriage. Skills gleaned from law books and courtroom trials have transferred naturally to lawmaking and campaigning, and notable achievements as a lawyer have led to success in the political arena. Not surprisingly, law has been the single most common occupation among members of the United States Senate, from the founding years to the present. It follows that how lawyers have practiced their profession should provide insights into how they would manage government.

Jack MacGregor Campbell has meticulously reconstructed Tennessee's first "trial of the century," a dramatic case that brought together shrewd and effective attorneys who would later serve in the United States Senate and emerge as national political leaders. The towering figures of Andrew Jackson, Thomas Hart Benton, and especially Felix Grundy, make this account more than a murder trial.

The trial offers insights into nineteenth-century sensibilities on the rough-and-tumble frontier. It shows how the legal system operated, how attorneys persuaded juries, how opinions were rendered, and how justice was served. The "Great Magness Trial" remains just as compelling now as it did when it attracted crowds of curious onlookers two centuries ago.

Donald A. Ritchie
Historian Emeritus, United States Senate

THE GREAT
MAGNESS TRIAL

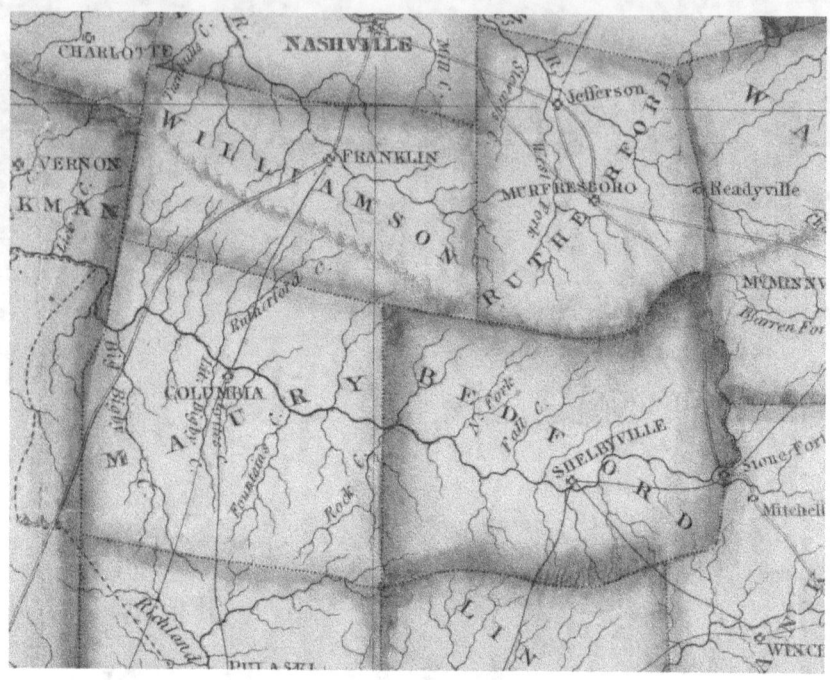

The Middle Tennessee counties of Williamson and Bedford where the events surrounding the Magness trial took place.

1

The Killing of Patton Anderson

On November 22, 1810, John Reid, future aide-de-camp and biographer of Andrew Jackson, wrote to his father from Franklin, Tennessee, "There is a very important criminal prosecution going on here now—that of the Magnesses for having murdered Patton Anderson."[1] Indeed, it was an important event. It became a legal experiment that tested the ability of jurors to carry out their duties in the face of powerful men seeking the conviction of the defendants.

The pertinent events seem straightforward at first glance. On Wednesday, October 24th, 1810, David Magness shot Major Patton Anderson through the heart in Shelbyville, Tennessee. Magness was

---

1. John Reid Papers, Volume 1, 1802-1842, Library of Congress MMC-3365.

quickly apprehended along with his father Jonathan and his brother Perrygreen and placed in the Davidson County jail.[2]

The victim, Patton Anderson, was well known in Tennessee. He was descended from one of the most respectable families in Virginia and was a long time close friend of Andrew Jackson.[3] At the time of the shooting, Anderson was a trusted captain under him in the militia and had raised and commanded at least one company of men for his corps.[4] He was also the brother of Jackson's aide-to-camp at the time, Colonel William Preston Anderson.

The turn of the nineteenth century was a violent and tempestuous time for the group of men that surrounded Andrew Jackson on America's western frontier. Not only had the settlers been in constant conflict with the Native American tribes that were being displaced, but "aggressiveness among young men was most persistent on the frontier, where violence begat violence."[5] According to one author, "men of the frontier felt the need to assert their strengths, indulge in profanity, and behave violently in order to conquer or deny their fears of the wilderness condition."[6] Histories of that era imply that there was general and perpetual intoxication among men on the Tennessee frontier and that "people in all walks of life engaged in duels and tavern brawls."[7]

By 1810, Andrew Jackson and his cabal were known to exhibit the short-tempered and violent proclivities of Tennessee frontiersmen. Jackson had barely arrived in Tennessee when he engaged in his first known duel. When trying a minor case in Jonesborough,

---

2. Tennessee Divorce, Probate, and Other Records 1800–1899. Tennessee County Records, Tennessee State Library and Archives, Williamson County, 1810. Miscellaneous Records (liquor licenses to slave records), Roll B-126: 329.

3. *Nashville Democratic Clarion*, November 2, 1810. Will T. Hale and Dixon L. Merritt, *A History of Tennessee and Tennesseans*. Volume III. New York, The Lewis Publishing Company, 1913, 838. James Phelan, *History of Tennessee: The Making of a State*. Boston: Houghton, Mifflin, and Company, 1888, 359.

4. Marquis James, *Andrew Jackson: the Border Captain*. New York: Grosset and Dunlap, 1933, 121–125.

5. Andrew Burstein, *The Passions of Andrew Jackson*. New York: Vintage Books, 2004, 17.

6. *Ibid*.

7. Robert Ewing Corlew, *Tennessee: A Short History*. Knoxville: The University of Tennessee Press, 113.

THE KILLING OF PATTON ANDERSON

Andrew Jackson was an ambitious lawyer, judge, and major general of the Tennessee state militia. His personal interest in the Magness trial stemmed from his friendship with the slain Patton Anderson. (Courtesy of the Library of Congress)

Jackson became enraged when his opposing counsel, Waightstill Avery, a man whom Jackson had sought out earlier as a mentor, apparently mocked him with sarcasm to ridicule a point he had made at bar.[8] Jackson "tore a leaf from a law book, scribbled a few lines on it, and hurled it" at the opposing counsel, challenging him to a duel. While his temper was fully displayed in the Avery affair, his violence was not. After the paces were walked and the signal was given, both men shot their pistols in the air avoiding bloodshed but nonetheless restoring Jackson's sense of honor.[9]

Between 1796 and 1803, Jackson feuded with John "Nolichuchy Jack" Sevier. He was collecting power and prestige during this period as he climbed the political rungs from member of the U.S. House of Representatives to senator and justice of the Tennessee Supreme Court. Sevier, a Revolutionary War hero and the first governor of the state, had among other things thwarted Jackson's first attempt to be elected commanding general of the Tennessee militia. Sevier was in his second stint as governor when Jackson challenged him to a duel in 1803.[10] The long-simmering tension between the two men had boiled over when in one encounter Sevier directed his insults past Jackson and towards Jackson's wife. When an encounter between the two men finally did take place, rushes were made and pistols were drawn but no shots were fired. The facts surrounding the fray were disputed between the camps.[11]

Many of the stories about Jackson's bad temper and violence involved carousing with, gambling with, or coming to the aid of a distressed or endangered Patton Anderson.[12] It was Anderson, for

---

8. Robert V. Remini, *Andrew Jackson and the Course of American Empire, 1767-1821*. New York: Harper and Row Publishers, 1977, 38-39.

9. *Ibid.*

10. Remini, *Andrew Jackson and the Course of American Empire*, 100-102, 117-125.

11. James, *Andrew Jackson: The Border Captain*, 85-94.

12. Burke Davis, *Old Hickory: A Life of Andrew Jackson*. New York: Dial Press, 1977, 62-63. James Parton, *Life of Andrew Jackson in Three Volumes*, 1: 342. James, *The Border Captain*, 142. Gary Alan Webb, "The Magness Trials." *Williamson County Historical Journal* 15 (1984). Cowdon, John B., Tennessee's Celebrated Case. 1958. Pages 19-20. James D. Anderson, *Making the American Thoroughbred; Especially in Tennessee 1800-1845*. Plimpton Press, 1916. Reprinted General Books Memphis Tennessee. 2010. Remini, *Andrew Jackson and the Course of American Empire*, 161-163.

instance, who was primarily responsible for causing the quarrel between Jackson and Charles Dickinson.[13] That quarrel, which is the most renowned of Jackson's fights, was related to wagers on the race between the horses Ploughboy and Truxton and led to a duel between the men. After the paces were taken, Jackson was shot in the chest, but remained poised, misfired, recocked his pistol, and killed Dickinson.[14] This 1806 duel damaged Jackson's reputation and his entourage as some considered his actions little more than murder.[15]

More than any member of Jackson's coterie, Patton Anderson was reputed to be a violent, aggressive, drinking man. This would be quite important legally. He was known "to associate with the wrong sort of people, and at times he was overbearing and belligerent."[16] Anderson "was a heavy drinker and a mean drunk" and "his violent temper continuously involved him in numerous quarrels and fights."[17] Such behavior would tend to shed a dim light on Anderson, the victim, and assist the Magnesses, the defendants, in the quest to be acquitted.

The newspaper account of his death delved into the bad reputation of Patton Anderson:

> Perhaps few men ever lived as publicly as Mr. Anderson whose character is difficult to sketch. Descended from one of the most respectable families in Virginia, he imbibed in early youth habits which in riper years he was the slave of. The worst of which were his uncontrollable passions, in the fury of which his native goodness of heart peeped out like the sun from behind a cloud and shed a luster over his failings; but a continual round of sporting often laid him open to knaves, who profiting by the confidence placed in them, plundered him of his wealth, and added strength to his ungovernable passions.[18]

13. *Correspondence of Andrew Jackson*, I, 129.

14. Thomas E. Watson, *The Life and Times of Andrew Jackson*. Thomson, GA: The Jeffersonian Publishing Company, 1912, 115–116.

15. Corlew, *Tennessee: A Short History*, 115.

16. Webb, "The Magness Trials," 21.

17. *Ibid.*

18. *Nashville Democratic Clarion*, November 2, 1810.

This description of Anderson in the Nashville newspaper of the day, the *Democratic Clarion*, also described the scene of the killing, but inaccurately reported that it was Perrygreen Magness who had pulled the trigger. This error has been perpetuated in many of the accounts of the trial that have been written.[19] The paper reported:

> On Wednesday the 24th ult. Mr. Patton Anderson was shot at Bedford courthouse, about one o'clock in the evening. The circumstances of the case is [sic] variously related, but it is believed the following account may be relied on. In the morning Jonathan Magness, the father, and Perrygreen Magness and David Magness, the sons, with others, who were at enmity with Anderson, were noticed to be engaged in a close conversation at a distance from any other company, and when they separated Perry M. had a holster of pistols on his arm, and a pair of saddle bags over them. After sauntering about some time they came to where Patton Anderson was—and the old man spoke to him about the subject of their difference, and a quarrel ensued. Anderson drew a dirk, on which a friend of his took hold of him and led him off a few steps, but they continued to use abusive words, until Perry M. who had seated himself at the far side of the house, walked up and shot Mr. Anderson through the heart.[20]

A Bedford County grand jury was quickly impaneled since the court already sat for the October 1810 term of the Circuit Court of the Fourth Circuit of Tennessee. The grand jury chose to indict David Magness for the murder of Patton Anderson and charged Perrygreen and Jonathan Magness with assisting and abetting David in the murder.[21] The grand jury indictment against David,

---

19. William N. Chambers, "Thomas Hart Benton in Tennessee," *Tennessee Historical Quarterly* 8:4 (1949),

20. *Nashville Democratic Clarion*, November 2, 1810.

21. State v. Jordan Reeves, Tennessee Divorce, Probate, and Other Records 1800–1899. Tennessee County Records. Tennessee State Library and Archives. Nashville, TN. Williamson County, 1810. Miscellaneous Records (liquor licenses to slave records) Roll B-126: 365.

The present-day Bedford County Courthouse in Shelbyville, Tennessee (Photograph by the author)

Perrygreen, and Jonathan Magness was signed by Fourth Circuit Solicitor General Alfred Balch. It read:

> They having not fear of God before their eyes, but being moved and seduced by the instigation of the Devil on the 24th day of October 1810 with force of arms at the county aforesaid in and upon one Patton Anderson in the peace of God and in the said State, then and there being feloniously, willfully, and with their malice aforethought did make an assault and that the said David Magness a certain pistol, value of ten dollars then and there loaded with gun powder and one leaden bullet which pistol he the said David Magness in his right hand then and there had and held to against and upon the said Patton Anderson, then and there did feloniously and of his malice aforethought did shoot and discharge, and that the said David Magness with the leaden bullet aforesaid out of the pistol aforesaid then and there by force of the gunpowder shot and sent forth as aforesaid the aforesaid Patton Anderson in and

upon the left side of him, the said Patton Anderson, a little below the left pap.[22]

The lead bullet from David Magness's pistol created, "one mortal wound of the depth of 4 inches and breadth of half an inch of which mortal wound Anderson then and there instantly died."[23] The indictment continued:

> Perrygreen (Perrygrren) Magness and Jonathan Magness then and there feloniously willfully and of their malice aforethought were present, aiding, helping, abetting, comforting, assisting, and maintaining the said David Magness.[24]

The indictment was endorsed by John Casey, the Bedford County prosecutor, and the Magnesses pleaded not guilty before the Bedford County Court, Fourth Circuit Judge Thomas Stuart on November 16, 1810.[25]

The Magnesses objected to being tried in Bedford County. They asked for a change of venue because "the murder charge is recent and the public mind is much inflamed against them" and "the connections and friends of the deceased are numerous and influential in Bedford County and they think they cannot be given a fair and impartial trial there."[26] Upon the motion of the Magnesses, the judge

---

22. *Ibid*, 366.

23. *Ibid*, 367.

24. *Ibid*. Williamson County, Tennessee Miscellaneous Records Volume 3: 49. Compiled by Louise Gillespie Lynch. 1980.

25. Judge Stuart had previously served as the federal prosecutor for the District of Tennessee from 1802 to 1803 and the District of Western Tennessee (when a division was made) from 1803 to 1810. He was the fourth person to have had that position. The Magness's antagonist, Andrew Jackson, was the first prosecuting attorney for the District of Tennessee having served from 1790 to 1797. The victim's brother, William P. Anderson, was the third person to have served in that position from 1798 to 1802. State *v.* Jordan Reeves. Tennessee Divorce, Probate, and Other Records 1800–1899. Tennessee County Records. Tennessee State Library and Archives. Nashville, TN. Williamson County, 1810. Miscellaneous Records (liquor licenses to slave records) Roll B-126: 368. See also Williamson County, Tennessee, Miscellaneous Records Volume 3: 49. Compiled by Louise Gillespie Lynch, 1980.

26. Williamson County, Tennessee, Miscellaneous Records Volume 3: 50. See also Nashville Clarion, November 2, 1810.

ordered that the trial would be held in Williamson County.[27] The trial was ordered to be held on the first Thursday after the second Monday of November 1810, at the Williamson County courthouse in Franklin, Tennessee.[28] Accordingly the trial began on November 12, 1810.

Preparing for the Trial

Soon after Patton Anderson was shot, his friends joined together to aid in the prosecution of the Magnesses. These friends—who included such prominent leaders as Andrew Jackson, Thomas Hart Benton, Jenkin Whiteside, and John Overton—"assembled to prosecute the case and see Magness hung."[29] It was said that Jackson in particular was "a warm and enthusiastic friend of Anderson, [who] spared no exertion to have Magness convicted."[30]

Four days after Anderson's death, on October 28, 1810, Overton wrote to John Coffee and outlined how the friends of Anderson could support the prosecution of the Magnesses. Overton was a lawyer and judge who was a close friend and adviser to Jackson and had succeeded him on the Superior Court of Tennessee.[31] Coffee was another friend and business partner of Jackson who had recently married the General's niece.[32] Overton provided his expert advice on how the prosecution should build its case.[33] He wrote, "Wm. P.A., the brother of deceased, is unfortunately absent. Every circumstance combines to tender if proper that I should pay atten-

27. Tennessee Divorce, Probate, and Other Records 1800–1899. Tennessee County Records. Tennessee State Library and Archives, Nashville, TN. Williamson County, 1810, Miscellaneous Records (liquor licenses to slave records) Roll B-126: 388 and 420.

28. John Overton to John Coffee, October 28, 1810. Dyas Collection of the John Coffee Papers, Tennessee Historical Society, Box 11, Folder 9.

29. Filson Club History Quarterly, Volume 47, No. 2 (April 1973), 174.

30. Phelan, *History of Tennessee*, 359.

31. S.G. Heiskell, *Andrew Jackson and Early Tennessee History*. Nashville: Ambrose Printing Company, 1918, 430.

32. In 1806, Coffee had also challenged Nathaniel A. McNairy to a duel for publishing derogatory statements about Jackson.

33. John Overton to John Coffee, October 28, 1810. Dyas Collection of the John Coffee Papers, Tennessee Historical Society, Box 11, Folder 9.

tion to this prosecution in his absence." He listed several "points I wish attended to" and described the need of the prosecution to produce a witness with particular credentials. The witness needed to be someone "who has the confidence of Old Magness and family and such of his neighbors as may have heard Old Magness or any of his fam[ily] converse respecting the quarrel of the Magnesses with Patton Anderson and take particular notice of it."

Overton continued, "If any person has heard either of the three Magnesses say anything [*illegible word*] or greedy they must be summoned by subpoena from Williamson." In an instruction brimming with coercion, he suggested that some "friend of Anderson must go with the Sherriff [*sic*] when he serves the subpoenas if the persons summoned are supposed to be friends of the Magnesses. I would recommend that the Sherriff [*sic*] should summon any persons who are friends of Magnesses." Overton wished that someone would go to John Drake and tell him to "get Tune the taylor [*sic*] from Lebanon who is a material witness" because "he may be in danger." Tune should be "sent to Mr. John Eaton in Fra[nklin]," who would "secure a place for him to stay until court and where he can be safe."[34] In the same letter, Overton noted that "some reputable man in Lebanon must be summoned to support the character of Tune should it be attacked—I am told that Tune is a man of good character and I suppose that Mr. Creitcher, Mr. Johnson, Doctor Hogg, or Mr. Rawlings can testify to this; any one of them will be sufficient."

Overton further stated:

> I will state the witnesses I have already got my eye on for the State, John Casey, Stephen Bedford, William Hamilton, Edward Cage, Edward Wade, Benjamin Bradford, William Tune, James Robertson, John Drake, John Hutchings, Lemmel Hutchings, John Coffee, John Bradley, Joseph Phillips, and John Griffin and Malcolm Gilchrist, John Eaton—I know nearly what all

---

34. John Eaton, another close friend of Jackson's, would be elected to the U.S. Senate in 1818 and later served as U.S. Secretary of War under President Jackson. Eaton was elected to the Senate at age 28 making him technically ineligible to serve. His eligibility, however, was not challenged and he stands in history as the youngest person to ever serve in the U.S. Senate.

John Coffee, close friend and business partner of Andrew Jackson (Courtesy of the Tennessee State Library and Archives)

these witnesses will state except Hamilton. If Mr. Drake or any of the friends of the deceased should find out any testimony beside the persons I have mentioned, they will let me know and the amount of their testimony."

Overton revealed the basic premise of the prosecution's case of conspiracy to commit murder:

> Testimony against Old Magness and Perry Magness are most material for the friends of the deceased to attest to. There is no doubt there was a combination to kill Anderson before [...*illegible marks*...] it took place, and any testimony that the friends of the deceased may hear of shewing malice or quarrel in the old man and his sons, against.

At this point, the rest of his thoughts are lost to either a missing page of the letter or an understanding that his reader would know how to complete them.

In the final page of Overton's letter to Coffee, he wrote that "Magness and his two sons must be attended to" and wished "to see John Drake in the course of a week or ten days, so as to arrange the testimony and prepare for trial."[35]

Before the trial began, Judge Stuart of the Fourth Circuit Court of Tennessee ordered the sheriff of Williamson County, William Hulme, to "immediately with a sufficient guard go to the jail of Davidson County" and take custody of the prisoners David Magness, Perrygreen Magness and Jonathan Magness. He was instructed "under safe and secure conduct forthwith [to] bring them before our said Circuit Court now sitting in at Franklin in the County of Williamson aforesaid to answer a charge against them for the murder of Patton Anderson."[36] The judge also ordered Davidson County sheriff Michael C. Dunn and jailer Edward D. Hobbs to release the three Magnesses from "the jail at Nashville" so they might be brought before the court to hear the charges against them.

---

35. John Overton to John Coffee, October 28, 1810. Dyas Collection of the John Coffee Papers, Tennessee Historical Society, Box 11, Folder 9.

36. Williamson County, Tennessee, Miscellaneous Records Volume 1: 48–49.

2

Lawyers of Great Promise

The trial of the Magnesses was set to begin in Franklin, Tennessee, on November 12, 1810. The accused hired Felix Grundy to represent them. Assisting Grundy in the defense were other prominent lawyers John Haywood and either O.B. Hayes, Andrew Hays, or Stockley Donelson Hays. John Overton supervised the hiring of some of Tennessee's best attorneys to aid the prosecution. The solicitor general for the Fourth Judicial Circuit, Alfred Balch, was joined by Jenkin Whiteside, Thomas Hart Benton, and Overton himself.

Felix Grundy

Destined for great prominence in the coming years, Felix Grundy had recently moved to Nashville in 1807 and set up a law practice. He would become "the first great criminal defense lawyer of the southern frontier" whose "mere appearance in a courtroom attracted spectators from miles around." He would also be one of the great political figures of his day and rank "with the greatest of the great of his time."[1]

Grundy was born in Berkeley County, Virginia, in 1777. He first moved with his parents to Brownsville, Pennsylvania, then to to Bardstown, Kentucky, in 1780. There he studied law and was admitted to the bar. He began his practice in Bardstown in 1797. Grundy served as a member of the Kentucky constitutional convention two years later. From 1800 to 1805, he served in the Kentucky House of Representatives. He was elected to the Kentucky Supreme Court of Errors and Appeals in 1808 and raised to Chief Justice the next year. Despite his meteoric rise in Kentucky law and politics, in the same year he became Chief Justice of Kentucky's highest court, Grundy resigned his position and moved to Tennessee.[2]

Some historians suggest Grundy left Kentucky to avoid conflict with Henry Clay and the growing political shadow cast by him.[3] Others speculate that he found the pay of the Supreme Court insufficient to support his growing family and left to disconnect entirely from public affairs.[4] For whatever reason, he removed to Tennessee in the winter of 1807–1808 and for several years thereafter devoted himself exclusively to the practice of law. It was said he had but few equals, and certainly no superiors.[5]

---

1. J. Roderick Heller III, *Democracy's Lawyer: Felix Grundy of the Old Southwest*. Baton Rogue: Louisiana State University Press, 2010, 2. Orval W. Batlor, "The Career of Felix Grundy, 1777–1840. An Address Before the Filson Club February 2, 1942." *The Filson Club Quarterly* 16:2 (April 1942), 102.

2. *Dictionary of American Biography*. Frances Howard Ewing, "The Senatorial Career of the Hon. Felix Grundy." *Tennessee Historical Magazine* 2 (October 1931), 3–27. *Ibid (January 1932)*, 2 (January 1932),111-35, 2 (April 1932): 220-24, 2 (July 1932): 270-91. Joseph Howard Parks, *Felix Grundy: Champion of Democracy*. Baton Rouge: Louisiana State University Press, 1940.

3. Baylor, "The Career of Felix Grundy," *The Filson Club Quarterly* 16:2 (April 1942), 96.

4. "Felix Grundy" in *Tennessee, The Volunteer State 1769–1923* 3. S.J. Clarke Publishing Company, 132.

5. Statement of Rep. A.V Brown of Tennessee in the House of Representatives. Congressional Globe, 26th Congress, 2nd Session, Vol. IX, 1841: 64.

Famous for his oratory skills, Felix Grundy served as Congressman, U.S. Senator, and Attorney General. (Courtesy of the U.S. Senate Historical Office)

According to Orval Baylor, the Magness trial was Grundy's first appearance before the Nashville bar.[6] It is hard to determine if this is absolutely true, but it is certain that the trial helped propel his career. He became legendary as a criminal defense attorney. One of his contemporaries, Judge Josephus Guild, wrote of him: "Felix Grundy will always rank among the greatest men this country has produced. He was Tennessee's greatest criminal advocate, and he was the peer of any the United States has produced."[7]

Grundy's political career in Tennessee was launched in earnest when he was elected to Congress on November 6, 1810. This was only six days before the first Magness trial began. He served in the Twelfth and Thirteenth Congresses from March 4, 1811, until his resignation in 1814. He was a member of the Tennessee House of Representatives from 1819-1825 and elected to the U.S. Senate in 1829 to fill the vacancy caused by the resignation of John H. Eaton. He was reelected in 1833 and served until July 4, 1838. At that time, Grundy resigned the Senate to accept the appointment of Attorney General in President Martin Van Buren's cabinet. He resigned in December 1839, having once again been elected to the Senate.[8] There he served until his death on December 19, 1840.[9]

In November 1810, it was legal rather than political help that the Magnesses needed and Grundy was the finest. The best description

---

6. Baylor, Orval W. The Career of Felix Grundy, 1777-1840. An address before the Filson Club February 2, 1942. The Filson Club Quarterly, Vol. 16 No. 2, April 1942. Louisville, KY: 98.

7. Guild, Jo. C., Old Times in Tennessee. Chapter XII – Felix Grundy – a reminiscence of the Great Tennessee Lawyer. Tavel, Eastman, and Howell, Nashville, TN, 1878: 293.

8. This election to the Senate, occurring on November 19, 1839, was to fill the vacancy caused by the resignation of Ephraim Foster. A question concerning Grundy's eligibility to be elected as Senator while holding the office of Attorney General of the United States was raised. Therefore, he resigned from the Senate on December 14, 1839, and was reelected by the Tennessee Legislature the same day and resumed his service.

9. This election to the Senate, occurring on November 19, 1839, was to fill the vacancy caused by the resignation of Ephraim Foster. A question concerning Grundy's eligibility to be elected as Senator while holding the office of Attorney General of the United States was raised. Therefore, he resigned from the Senate on December 14, 1839, was reelected by the Tennessee Legislature the same day, and resumed his service. Dictionary of American Biography; Ewing, Frances Howard. "The Senatorial Career of the Hon. Felix Grundy." Tennessee Historical Magazine 2 (October 1931): 3-27, 2 (January 1932): 111-35, 2 (April 1932): 220-24, 2 (July 1932): 270-91; Parks, Joseph. Felix Grundy: Champion of Democracy. Baton Rouge: Louisiana State University Press, 1940.

of Grundy's courtroom acumen comes from the reminiscence of Judge Guild in his 1878 book *Old Times in Tennessee*. Guild wrote:

> ...to hear Felix Grundy in a closely contested case of homicide, when all his fires were burning, his passions aroused; to see his actions, the flash of his gray eyes, the vivid flashes of lightning bursting from his lips; at times to witness his scathing sarcasm, and then his sparkling wit: take it all in all, it was the grandest exhibition than any Tennessean ever witnessed... I have heard Felix Grundy speak a hundred times. If he were alive I would go a thousand miles to hear him again.[10]

In November 1810, the Magnesses needed an advocate with the jury selection and probative skills of Felix Grundy. According to Orval Baylor, "Everybody of any consequence in Tennessee in Grundy's time recognized him as the outstanding criminal lawyer of the whole Southwest." It would become a common saying in Tennessee that "if Grundy can't save you, nobody can."[11] The Magness trial was going to be one of the first great trials—if not *the* first—upon which Grundy would build this reputation.

John Haywood

John Haywood was the attorney who opened the defense in the trial of David Magness. A lawyer, judge, and historian, he was born in Halifax County, North Carolina, in either 1753 or 1762. He was the son of Egbert Haywood, a "gallant officer in the Revolution," and is purported to have served himself on the staff of a North Carolina officer.[12]

Haywood was the Attorney General of North Carolina from 1791 to 1794. According to Col. A.S. Colyar, "such was his popularity, and

---

10. Id. at 83-84.
11. Baylor at 98.
12. Trial notes of John Reid, John Reid papers, 1802-1842, Library of Congress MMC-3365: 31. "John Haywood." Tennessee, The Volunteer State 1769-1923. Vol. II., S.J. Clarke Publishing Company, 142. Colyar, Col. A.S. "Sketch of the Author". Haywood, John. Civil and Political History of Tennessee. Publishing House of the Methodist Episcopal Church, South, 1891: 5.

so high was the estimate put on him by the bar of North Carolina, that after serving something over three years as Attorney-general, he was transferred to the bench and for ten or twelve years he was on the bench of the Superior Court of North Carolina."[13]

During that time, Haywood published a compilation of the laws of North Carolina, decisions of the Superior Court from 1789 to 1806, and a treatise on laws called *Haywood's Justice*.[14] He resigned his seat on the North Carolina court in 1800 to defend a friend, North Carolina Secretary of State James Glasgow, who was charged with forging land warrants.[15] The unpopularity of his client and the taint of his defense are cited as the main reasons that, sometime between 1804 and 1810, Haywood moved to Tennessee.[16] Various biographies of Haywood disagree on the year he arrived, but court records of the Magness trial place him there by October 1810.[17]

Haywood was elected to the Tennessee Supreme Court in 1812 and remained on the court for the next twenty-four years until his death in 1826.[18] In addition to serving as the accepted presiding judge of the Supreme Court, he engaged in various scholarly pursuits.[19] Judge Haywood established an informal law school at his home and wrote several books, including *The Natural and Aboriginal History of Tennessee, The Christian Advocate*, and his best known work, *The Civil and Political History of Tennessee*.[20]

Most of the commentary on Haywood's career focused on his role as a jurist. It was said that "he presided without any great amount

13. Id.

14. "John Haywood." Tennessee, The Volunteer State 1769-1923. Vol. II., S.J. Clarke Publishing Co.:142-143.

15. Col. A.S. Colyar, Civil and Political History of Tennessee. Publishing House of the Methodist Episcopal Church, South, 1891, 6.

16. "John Haywood." Tennessee, The Volunteer State 1769-1923. Vol. II., S.J. Clarke Publishing Co.:143.

17. Trial notes of John Reid, John Reid papers, 1802-1842., Library of Congress MMC-3365: 31.

18. Colyar, Col. A.S. Civil and Political History of Tennessee. Publishing House of the Methodist Episcopal Church, South, 1891: 6.

19. "John Haywood." Tennessee, The Volunteer State 1769-1923. Vol II., S.J. Clarke Publishing Co.:143.

20. Id.

*Judge John Haywood, Tennessee's "greatest and most learned jurist."
(Courtesy of the North Carolina Museum of History)*

of dignity, but commanded respect by his known superiority."[21] He was described as "the very model of a lawyer" and "a man of great sympathy and warm feeling" who "always leaned to the oppressed."[22] However, he was seemingly sharp with the advocates before him. According to one biographer:

> He possessed inexhaustible stores of imagination, and was quick in argument and in reply, but his imaginative faculties were so largely developed as to give to some of his opinions an air of eccentricity. Like most men of strong and quick minds and positive convictions, Haywood was sometimes regarded as overbearing. Is it said also that he was ambitious and was disposed to prefer his own judgments to those of his associates. This last characteristic is not at all exceptional in great judges.[23]

Of Haywood, it was written that he was Tennessee's "greatest and most learned jurist, and was esteemed by some the equal of Grundy as an advocate." His skills as a lawyer before the court "deserved high praise" and "in tact and eloquence—such eloquence as reaches the heart and convinces the judgment—Haywood had no equal in Tennessee."

The 350-pound Haywood died on December 12, 1826.[24]

Hayes or Hays?

In a letter dated November 17, 1810, Patton Anderson's brother, William Preston Anderson, gave Andrew Jackson an update on the Magness trial. "I don't altogether like the jury—Grundy and Hays

---

21. Colyar, Col. A.S. Civil and Political History of Tennessee. Publishing House of the Methodist Episcopal Church, South, 1891: 6.

22. "John Haywood." Tennessee, The Volunteer State 1769-1923. Vol II., S.J. Clarke Publishing Co.: 144. Colyar, Col. A.S. Civil and Political History of Tennessee. Publishing House of the Methodist Episcopal Church, South, 1891: 7.

23. "John Haywood." Tennessee, The Volunteer State 1769-1923. Vol II., S.J. Clarke Publishing Co.:143.

24. Id.

was guilty of a most ungentlemanlike and in fact rascally act in packing some of them."[25]

Aside from this mention by Anderson, there are only two surviving records in contemporary documents or court records of the trials of a Hays or Hayes that aided in the defense of the Magnesses. A "Question by Hayes" to "Phillips" is recorded in the notes of John Reid during the early stages of the trial.[26] Likewise, the efforts of opposition counsel, "Mr. Hayes," are described contemptuously by the prosecution attorneys during a discussion of the veracity of the testimony of Jordan Reeves.[27]

Editorial notes in the *Papers of Andrew Jackson*[28] and one history of the town of Franklin, Tennessee, identify him as Stockley Donelson Hays.[29] However, this seems unlikely as Stockley Hays was the nephew of Rachel Jackson and squarely in the orbit and under the influence of the anti-Magness cabal. So close was Stockley Hays to Andrew and Rachel Jackson that in 1811, he married Jackson's ward, Lydia Butler. On the same day, Stockley's sister, Patsy Hays, married Lydia's brother Dr. William E. Butler, who was also a ward of the Jacksons.[30]

It is possible that the Hays described by William Preston Anderson was Andrew Hays. In a speech to the Nashville Bar in 1876, Judge Josephus C. Guild listed Andrew Hays with Whiteside and

25. The Papers of Andrew Jackson, Volume II, 1829. University of Tennessee Press. Knoxville, TN, 2007: 255-256.

26. Trial notes of John Reid, John Reid papers, 1802-1842., Library of Congress MMC-3365: 10.

27. Id. at 31.

28. The Papers of Andrew Jackson, Volume II, 1829. University of Tennessee Press. Knoxville, TN 2007: 255.

29. Crutchfield, James A. and Holladay, Robert. Franklin -- Tennessee's Handsomest Town. Hillsboro Press, Franklin, TN 1999: 67.

30. Cheatham, Mark R. Andrew Jackson Southerner. Louisiana State University Press. Baton Rouge, LA, 2013: 55. Two other prominent sources discussing Stockley Donelson Hays and his family make no mention of Stockley Donelson Hays as an attorney in such a celebrated murder case. Judge John A. Pitts, the law partner of Hays' son, also named Stockley Donelson Hays, discussed the family in his work, *Personal and Professional Reminiscences of an Old Lawyer*, Southern Publishers, Inc., Kingsport, Tennessee 1930. Further, historian Emma Inman Williams, in her work, *Historic Madison: The Story of Jackson and Madison County, Tennessee from Mound Builders to World War I*, discusses the elder Hays in some great detail throughout various sections of the work, McCowat-Mercer Press, Jackson, Tennessee, 1946.

Grundy as being part of a "galaxy of talent that has never been excelled at any bar in these United States."[31] Guild refers to Andrew Hays merely as "Hays" throughout his speech without fear that his audience might confuse the "Hays" of this Nashville Bar Association pantheon with any other lawyers.[32]

Based on the circumstances, and the spelling in the notes from the trial itself, it is possible that the lawyer described in Anderson's letter is O.B. Hayes. Hayes moved to Nashville in 1808 after previously studying law in Baltimore. Henry Foote wrote of O.B. Hayes in 1876:

> ….by some he was very highly admired, and I have heard one or two of his efforts—especially in the defense of persons charged with crime—very high lauded.[33]

Jenkin Whiteside

From the time of his arrival in Middle Tennessee, Grundy's principal adversary before the courts was Jenkin Whiteside.[34] Whiteside "led the bar" of the area and the Magness trial may have been the first time Grundy battled Whiteside in court in a high profile trial.[35] He was known to be "a specialist in land law and settled many land controversies, especially those pertaining to academies and colleges."[36] He was also "devoted much to money making, and espe-

---

31. Guild, Josephus Conn. Old times in Tennessee: Historical, Personal, and Political Scraps and Sketches. Tavel, Eastman, and Howell, 1878: 340-342.

32. Id. at 337 through 346.

33. Foote, Henry S. The Bench and Bar of the South and Southwest. Soule, Thomas and Wentworth. St. Louis, MO, 1876: 162.

34. A short but very sufficient biographical sketch of Jenkin Whiteside can be found in the late Tennessee Senator Kenneth McKellar's biographical history of his predecessors in the United States Senate from Tennessee entitled Tennessee Senators As Seen By One Of Their Successors, Southern Publishers, Inc., Kingsport, Tennessee, 1942. "Jenkin Whiteside," Tennessee, The Volunteer State, Vol. II. SJ Clarke Publishing Co., 1923: 258.

35. Heller, J. Roderick, III. Democracy's Lawyer: Felix Grundy of the Old Southwest. Louisiana State University Press, Baton Rouge, LA, 2010: 85.

36. Foster, A.P. Assistant Librarian and Archivist. State of Tennessee Department of Education, Division of Library and Archives. Notes transmitted to the Congress of the United States,

cially delighting in what was known as speculation in uncultivated lands."³⁷ In addition, he was "a criminal lawyer of great renown."³⁸ During the first decade of the nineteenth century, it was thought he had the largest practice in the state of Tennessee.³⁹ In addition, Whiteside had also been elected to the U.S. Senate to fill a vacancy on April 11, 1809, and served from May 20, 1809, until October 8, 1811, when he resigned to resume the full-time practice of law. He was, therefore, a sitting U.S. Senator when the Magness trials began.⁴⁰

Whiteside was born in or near Lancaster, Pennsylvania in 1772. He grew up in the country near Lancaster and, when he turned eighteen, he moved to Lancaster proper to train to be a lawyer. There he realized he was not ready to practice law and soon procured a position at the University of Pennsylvania to prepare himself for his chosen craft.⁴¹ Whiteside reportedly had great difficulty at the university, experiencing privations, struggles, and disappointments.⁴² After graduation and with the help of an admiring university president, he obtained a position as the head of an academy in Trenton, New Jersey. He stayed there for some years, saving money before resigning, walking to Philadelphia and traveling by boat to Richmond, Virginia.

In Richmond, Whiteside sought the tutelage of John Marshall, who would become the fourth Chief Justice of the United States in 1801. Marshall took a great interest in Whiteside and secured for him a teaching position at an academy in order to help him make a living while studying law. Marshall challenged Whiteside and forced

---

Joint Committee on Printing. March 1926. Senate Historian's Office. Biographical file of Senator Jenkin Whiteside. Washington, DC.

37. Foote, Henry S. The Bench and Bar of the South and Southwest, Soule, Thomas and Wentworth, St. Louis, 1876: 159.

38. McKellar, Kenneth. Tennessee Senators, As Seen by One of Their Successors. Southern Publishers Inc., Kingsport, Tenn., 1942: 124.

39. Foster, A.P. Assistant Librarian and Archivist. State of Tennessee Department of Education, Division of Library and Archives. Notes transmitted to the Congress of the United States, Joint Committee on Printing. March 1926. Senate Historian's Office. Biographical file of Senator Jenkin Whiteside. Washington, DC.

40. Id.

41. McKellar at 124.

42. Id. at 122.

him to endure some degree of academic tribulation, but eventually allowed him to prepare bills of equity and perform other legal work.

Having trained under Marshall for some extent of time, Whiteside eventually obtained a license to practice law and moved to Wytheville, Virginia, to set up a practice. He apparently didn't like Wytheville, so he continued west and settled in Knoxville, Tennessee, in 1795 or 1796.[43]

Whiteside practiced law in Knoxville for some time. He was one of the town commissioners in 1801 and 1802 and stayed there until 1808 or 1809.[44] Whether he moved his home and practice to Nashville to be closer to river transportation to Washington, D.C., or to be near the Supreme Court of Tennessee is not known, but he was elected to the U.S. Senate in 1809. Reports of the Supreme Court show he was "the most active lawyer of his time in Tennessee from 1811 to 1822"[45] and that "his most frequent competitor, after 1808, was Felix Grundy."[46]

As a trial lawyer, Whiteside was described as being "of a rough and unimposing exterior; of awkward and ungainly manners," and having "no relish whatever for those elegant and refined pursuits which are understood to distinguish polished and aristocratic communities." This "course [sic] and unpretending cordiality…made him many friends and no enemies."[47]

Whiteside was known for his level of detailed preparation and intense study and consideration of details. The *Nashville Constitutional Advocate* in 1822 remarked that he approached a trial "like a gladiator who was anointed for the combat and had descended into the arena."

> When he was for a plaintiff he attended to the most minute matters which might promote his success. He gathered up

---

43. Id. at 123.
44. Id. at 124.
45. Id. at 122.
46. "Jenkin Whiteside." Tennessee, The Volunteer State, Vol. II. SJ Clarke Publishing Co., 1923: 258.
47. Foote, Henry S. The Bench and Bar of the South and Southwest, Soule, Thomas and Wentworth, St. Louis, MO, 1876: 160.

and marshaled his facts with the greatest judgment and most discriminating skill. He not only erected his fortification but added breast works and ditches and every means of defense.[48]

It was said of Whiteside that "his greatest excellence lay in the strength of his reasoning powers" and "if any abstruse proposition were stated to him, his mind seemed to take the alarm, and to view it with doubt and hesitation." His strength as a lawyer rested in his ability to offer truth or attack falsity "by a course of close logical and irresistible arguments." Once convinced of the correctness of his position, "he sustained it with such power that he was not to be beaten by any man, no matter how learned or dexterous or powerful he might be in an intellectual combat." It was this ability to reason which led to the opinion of him that "on a cross examination of a doubtful witness he was wholly unrivalled" in the courts of Tennessee.[49]

Jenkin Whiteside died in Nashville on September 25, 1822, at the age of fifty.

John Overton

Judge John Overton was a prominent man in early Tennessee history. He was among the earliest Supreme Court judges of the state, one of the founders of Memphis, and known as Andrew Jackson's "earliest friend and most intimate associate."[50] He was the member of Jackson's inner circle "more trusted by the deeply suspicious Jackson than any other" and had "self-assumed" a role "to shield his general from the wicked and to lash back at enemies when appropriate."[51] In 1810, the Magnesses were the enemies.

Overton was born in Louisa County, Virginia, on April 9, 1766. He acquired what was described as a "good education" through self

---

48. McKellar, 125.

49. Ibid, 124-125.

50. Benton, Thomas H. Thirty Years View. Vol. I, Greenwood Press Publishers. New York, NY, 1968: 738

51. Ratner, Lorman A. Andrew Jackson and His Tennessee Lieutenants, Greenwood Press. Westport, CT, 1997: 35.

instruction and apparently taught school at some point, using his salary to purchase books.[52] Following the Revolutionary War, Overton migrated to Kentucky where one or more of his brothers already lived; he had two elder brothers who were veterans of the war.[53]

In 1789, Overton moved to the bustling town of Nashville with the credentials of a lawyer. He established his law practice as well as a mercantile partnership and boarded at the home of Rachel Donelson, a well-respected woman and the widow of John Donelson." It was here that Overton would come to know Andrew Jackson. Jackson also boarded with the widow Donelson and shared a room and bed with Overton. Their friendship would remain strong for the next thirty-six years and Overton became Jackson's counselor and advisor. He provided Jackson with political organizational skills, as well as money, having become wealthy from his activities as a land speculator.[54]

As Overton built his legal practice, he assumed various government roles. He received a commission as a federal revenue inspector from President Washington and held that position until 1808. In 1803, he was appointed Tennessee's representative on a commission to settle land disputes between Tennessee, North Carolina, and the federal government.[55]

When Jackson resigned his position as one of the judges of the Tennessee Superior Court, Overton was appointed to the seat. He remained a judge on the Superior Court until it was abolished under the court reform legislation that became effective in early 1810. A year later, he was appointed by the state legislature to the successor court, the Supreme Court of Errors and Appeals, and remained

---

52. Heiskell, S.G. Andrew Jackson and Early Tennessee History, Ambrose Printing Co., Nashville, TN, 1918: 429.

53. Ratner at 36.

54. Ibid. John Overton once owned the land upon which Memphis now stands. He had purchased 500 acres of property at Chickasaw Bluff from a man named Elijah Rice for $5,000. At some point Andrew Jackson and General James Winchester held an interest in this land as well, and together they conveyed the property to the creation of the town of Memphis. Overton laid out the town in 1820.

55. Ratner, 36.

John Overton
(Courtesy of Historic Travellers Rest Plantation and Museum)

in that position until April 11, 1816.[56] It was between his stints as a Supreme Court judge that the Magness trials began.

Overton would remain the loyal and trusted friend of Jackson the rest of his life. He played an important role in encouraging him to run for public office. For his benefit, he created the "Nashville Committee," essentially a campaign committee that served Jackson throughout his political career. Overton remained a key advisor on political and policy issues during his presidency, one to whom Jackson would consult in times of crisis and scandal.[57]

Despite Overton's acumen as a judge, there is little to indicate how he performed as a trial advocate or his experience with juries. He is listed as an advocate for the prosecution of the Magnesses in many histories of the trial, yet his principal roles seemed to be that of legal labor organizer and support for the prosecution.

John Overton died at "Traveller's Rest," his home in Nashville, on April 12, 1833.[58]

Thomas Hart Benton

When the trial was moved to Franklin, the Jackson-Overton cabal hired a young local attorney named Thomas Hart Benton to assist in the prosecution. Though relatively unknown in 1810, he eventually attained great fame, prestige, and power. It was his association with the Magness trial that first attached Benton to Andrew Jackson, who, in turn, would be the original source of Benton's rise as an American statesman.

Benton was born at Hart's Hill near Hillsborough in Orange County, North Carolina, on March 14, 1782. His father, Jesse Benton, was a lawyer with large land holdings in North Carolina, Kentucky, and Tennessee. His mother, Ann (Gooch) Benton, was "a woman of force, and, for her time, of much education." Jesse died in the winter of 1790–91, leaving some 20,000 acres to his heirs.[59]

---

56. Heiskell, 430. Ratner, 37.

57. Heiskell, 430, 431, 433. Ratner, 37.

58. Speed, Thomas. The Political Club, John P. Morton and Co., Louisville, KY, 1894: 88

59. "Thomas Hart Benton", Tennessee, The Volunteer State, Vol. II, S.J. Clarke Publishing Co., 1923: 27. Powell, William S., ed. Dictionary of North Carolina Biography, Vol. 2, D-G.,

After the Magness trial, Thomas Hart Benton became a towering figure in U.S. politics. (Courtesy of the Library of Congress)

Thomas Hart Benton began his education at home where according to Theodore Roosevelt, his mother "began the training of her son's mind, studying with him history and biography." His studies continued at a grammar school taught by a young New England educator of "good ability."[60] Shortly after Christmas 1798, he entered the University of North Carolina at Chapel Hill, but left in disgrace less than three months later after confessing to stealing money from his roommates. He returned home and never graduated.[61]

In 1801, Benton's mother moved the family to one of the tracts of land left to them by Jesse, a 2,560-acre tract near Leiper's Fork, Tennessee, about 25 miles southwest of Nashville. There he taught school and began studying for a career in the law. Of Benton, Theodore Roosevelt described him as an "insatiable student and reader" who "rapidly acquired a very extensive knowledge, not only of law, but of history and even of Latin and English literature, and thus became a well-read and cultivated, indeed a learned man." He was admitted to practice law at Franklin in 1806.[62]

As Benton built his legal career, he also sought to establish himself politically. He was elected to the state senate and served from 1809 to 1811. There he sponsored a number of bills, including one that resulted in the establishment of the circuit court system in Tennessee. Another guaranteed that slaves had the right to a trial by jury in matters outside the jurisdiction of their masters.[63]

Benton's record as a lawyer is thin when compared to his political career as he was "from the first much fonder of political pursuits than of the study of law-books."[64] He was involved in some forty-five cases from the fall of 1810 to the middle of 1812.[65] His practice

---

University of North Carolina Press, Chapel Hill, NC, 1979: 139. Roosevelt, Theodore, Thomas Hart Benton, Houghton Mifflin and Co., Boston and New York, 1886: 24. Powell at 139.

60. Roosevelt at 24.

61.   Powell at 139.

62. Ibid. Roosevelt at 25. Chambers, William Nisbet. Old Bullion Benton, Senator from the New West. Little Brown and Co., Boston, Mass., 1956: 22-24.

63. Id. at 33 and 34. Id. at 34.

64. Foote, Henry S. The Bench and Bar of the South and Southwest. Soule, Thomas and Wentworth, St. Louis, MO, 1876: 160.

65. Chambers at 35.

was varied as he rode the circuit in central Tennessee. Citing Benton's notes from this era, William Chambers wrote:

> The causes of action in which lawyer Benton was involved were ramified: slander, trove, divorce, suits in equity, land conveyances, trespass, ejectment, assault and battery, all were in his ken and grist for his legal mill. And while he did most of his business in his home county, he also traveled through the woods and over the dirt roads to Bedford, Maury, Rutherford, Giles, Dickson, Hickman, and his own legislative child, Lincoln.[66]

Though Benton was more interested in a political career than a legal one, ironically it would be a case in the law, the Magness trial, which would give Benton his path to political power. The Magness trial brought Benton into the orbit of Andrew Jackson. In his autobiographical book, Benton wrote of the Magness trial:

> I was employed in a criminal case of great magnitude, where the oldest and the ablest counsel appeared – Haywood, Grundy, Whiteside, —and the trial of which General Jackson attended through concern for the fate of a friend. As junior counsel, I had to precede my elders, and did my best; and, it being on the side of his feelings, he found my effort to be better than it was. He complimented me greatly, and from that time our intimacy began.[67]

Following the Magness trial, Benton's relationship with Jackson transformed. Previously it had been an acquaintance and a men-

---

66. Chambers, William Nisbet. Thomas Hart Benton in Tennessee 1801-1812. Tennessee Historical Quarterly, Vol. VIII, December 1949, Number 4: 328. Lincoln County was established on November 14, 1809 by an Act sponsored by Benton. The county is named for Revolutionary War hero General Benjamin Lincoln.

67. Benton at 736.

tor/protégé relationship but matured into an intimate friendship in which Benton was a welcome guest at the Hermitage.[68]

When war commenced between Britain and the United States in 1812, Benton was elected Colonel of the Second Regiment of Tennessee Volunteers and Jackson, the commanding general of the Tennessee militia, named him as his aide-de-camp.[69] Benton accompanied Jackson on his expedition to Natchez in 1813 and on the famous return march back to Tennessee where Jackson was given the nickname "Old Hickory" for enduring the hardships of the march with his men. Tough though he was, the War Department had specifically ordered Jackson to disband his troops at Natchez and having disobeyed this command, Jackson was personally liable to the Army Quartermaster for $12,000 in costs related to the return march to Nashville.[70] After their return to Nashville, Benton was preparing to travel to Washington, D.C. to obtain an appointment in the regular Army. Presumably at the request of Jackson, while he was in Washington, Benton lobbied the government to cover the costs of the return march. Benton was able to spare Jackson the burden of repaying the Quartermaster the crippling sum, and was also successful in obtaining a commission as a Lieutenant Colonel in the newly organized southern Army.[71]

Upon his return he learned of an event that would create a division between him and his benefactor, and still commanding officer, Andrew Jackson. Jackson had stood as second to a man named William Carroll in a duel with Jesse Benton, the brother of Thomas Hart Benton. Jackson biographer Thomas E. Watson wrote:

"Thus the strange spectacle was presented of one of the Benton brothers striving heroically to save Jackson from ruin in Washington, while the other was risking his life in a combat with pistols, with Jackson on the other side."[72]

---

68. Chambers, William Nisbet. "Thomas Hart Benton in Tennessee 1801-1812". Tennessee Historical Quarterly, Vol. VIII, December 1949, Number 4: 330.

69. Powell at 140.

70. Heiskell at 333.

71. Id.

72. Watson, Life and Times of Andrew Jackson, The Jeffersonian Publishing Co., Thomson, Georgia, 1912: 141.

When Thomas Hart Benton learned of Jackson's role in the duel he was furious. According to Watson:

> The situation seemed to Col. Tom Benton so unnatural, so outrageous, so ungrateful, so tantalizing, and intolerable, that he, being a man of fierce temper and fearless disposition himself, began to denounce Jackson's conduct in unmeasured language.[73]

Hearing of Benton's angry words, Jackson swore that he would "horse-whip" Benton the first time he "ran across" him.[74] When Jackson did come across Benton again, he threatened Benton, horse whip-in hand, and things escalated to a gunfight. Jackson was shot and nearly bled to death.[75] The bullet shattered the bone in Jackson's left arm but Jackson refused the advice of most of his doctors to have the arm amputated. Jackson carried the bullet where it had lodged in his shoulder until 1831 when it was removed.[76] After the fight with Jackson, Benton was appointed Lieutenant Colonel in the regular Army of the United States and left Tennessee. After the war, he moved to St. Louis, Missouri.

From his new home, Benton was able to launch the political career for which he is known. In Missouri he began editing the (St. Louis) *Missouri Inquirer* and continued the practice of law.[77] On the day Missouri entered the Union, August 10, 1821, he was elected to be the first United States Senator from the state.[78] He was reelected to the Senate in 1827, 1833, 1839, and 1845, but the State Legislature denied him reelection in 1850.[79] He then turned to the people and was elected in 1852 to serve in the House of Representatives for the

---

73. Id.
74. Meigs, William Montgomery. The Life of Thomas Hart Benton. J.B. Lippincott Co., Philadelphia, PA, 1904: 76.
75. Burstein, Andrew. The Passions of Andrew Jackson. Vintage Books, New York, NY, 2004: 96.
76. Watson at 143.
77. Powell at 139.
78. Kennedy, John F. Profiles in Courage Memorial Edition, Harper and Row, 1964: 102.
79. Chambers at 368.

Thirty-third Congress.[80] He therefore served in the Senate from August 10, 1821 until March 3, 1851 and in the House from March 4, 1853 until March 3, 1855. He ran unsuccessfully for reelection to the House in 1854 and for governor of Missouri in 1856.[81]

Thomas Hart Benton was a towering political figure of the mid-nineteenth century. He somewhat ironically became a lead defender of President Jackson's policies, and was centrally involved in the major debates of his era. He led the fight in the Senate against the Bank of the United States and was a dedicated "hard money" advocate. His leadership and advocacy that "the government was to receive nothing but gold and silver for its revenues, and it should be kept by its own officers in real, not constructive, treasuries" earned him the moniker "Bullion Benton."[82] He was a leader in the fight for American expansion and development in the West and settlement of the Oregon Territory. According to Senator John F. Kennedy:

"The Pony Express, the telegraph line and the highways to the interior were among his proud accomplishments – and a transcontinental railroad and fully developed West were among his dreams."[83]

Though Thomas Hart Benton had, from 1821 to 1844, "reigned Supreme as Kingpin of Missouri politics, her first Senator, and beloved idol," his position on the great issues of the day, nullification and slavery, would put him at odds with his constituents and ultimately cost him his Senate seat.[84] He fought bitterly against nullification and the Compromise of 1850. While Benton was a slaveholder and one of the very few members of the Congress who still kept his slaves in his Washington household, he believed that the debate over slavery was an impediment to western expansion and he was resolutely opposed to the secessionists in the Senate. This opposition raised the ire of his fellow Southerners and especially of John

---

80. Id. at 387.
81. Powell at 141.
82. Roosevelt at 178.
83. Kennedy at 103.
84. Id. at 102.

C. Calhoun who worked with pro-slavery politicians and newspapers in Missouri to have Benton defeated in 1850.[85]

Thomas Hart Benton died on April 10, 1858.

Alfred Balch

Thomas Hart Benton's leadership in the creation of the circuit court system in Tennessee, as well as his patronage, helped launch the career of a young man of the Cumberland area named Alfred Balch. Under the new system, the Fourth District Circuit Court was authorized on November 16, 1809.[86] This circuit included Bedford County where the Magnesses were apprehended and Williamson County where they would be tried. For Alfred Balch, who was serving as the appointed solicitor for the Fourth Circuit at the time, the Magness trial would be a career altering experience, and would set him on a path to prominence and a future Presidential appointment.

Alfred Balch was born on September 17, 1785 at Georgetown in what would become the District of Columbia in 1790.[87] He attended Princeton College and graduated with the class of 1805 with an Artium Magister or Master's Degree.[88] Balch made his way to Tennessee and set up a legal practice in Nashville. Less than four years after his graduation from Princeton, the Fourth District Circuit Court was authorized in 1809 and Thomas Hart Benton, as his state Senator, secured for Balch the appointment as the first state solicitor for the new Circuit.[89] Balch was serving as the solicitor for

---

85. Id. at 101-120.

86. Hale, Will T. and Merritt, Dixon L. A History of Tennessee and Tennesseans, Vol. III, The Lewis Publishing Co., Chicago and New York, 1913: 838.

87. Balch, Thomas Willing. Balch Genealogical. Allen, Lane, and Scott, Philadelphia, PA, 1907: 206.

88. Id. at 207.

89. Hale, Will T. and Merritt, Dixon L. A History of Tennessee and Tennesseans, Vol. III, The Lewis Publishing Co., Chicago and New York, 1913: 838. Chambers at 34.

less than a year when Patton Anderson was shot. He served as solicitor until 1815.[90]

There is little on the record of Balch as a courtroom attorney. During the Magness trials his name and signature were prominent in the pleadings and motions, and there are notes of his orations before the court.[91] We do know that over the years in Nashville, Balch "shared in the area's prosperity" and "he developed a plantation, gaining as a neighbor Andrew Jackson."[92] He began speculating in land as was the norm of his day and place and engaged in the business and politics of banking.[93]

His relationship with Jackson, and no doubt his relationship with his mentor, now Missouri Senator Thomas Hart Benton, aided Balch in developing a federal career. In 1827, Balch was appointed by the Treasury Department as a special agent for the sale of some disputed land in the western District of Tennessee and in Georgia.[94] In 1829, Balch was on the short list to be the United States Attorney for the Western District of Tennessee. Secretary of State and future President Martin Van Buren corresponded with President Andrew Jackson about who best to appoint as the United States Attorney in Nashville. Jackson wrote to Van Buren:

> …respecting the appointment at Nashville (attorney) I shall leave that to you; fair reciprocity is always right, and as I have given you, in your State, a Collector, I leave you, in mine, to give us an attorney.

---

90. Miller, Chas. A. Official and Political Manual of the State of Tennessee. Marshall and Bruce Stationers, Nashville, TN, 1890: 188.

91. "Trial notes of John Reid." John Reid Papers, 1802-1842. Library of Congress MMC-3365: 165-171.

92. Manley, Walter W., The Supreme Court of Florida and Its Predecessor Courts 1821-1917. University of Florida Press, 1997: 84.

93. Heller, J. Roderick III. Democracy's Lawyer: Felix Grundy of the Old Southwest. Louisiana State University Press, Baton Rouge, LA, 2010: 116, 133 and 142.

94. U.S. Congress. House of Representatives Report C.C. —No. 263, "Report of the US Court of Claims to the House of Representatives re: C.J Jenkins and WW Mann, Assignees of John McKinnie." Thirty-Sixth Congress, Second Session, 1860–61 (December 18,1860), 27–32, 42.

Jackson also told Van Buren that he would direct all the recommendations for the position to him. Two recommendations were sent to Van Buren: Balch and James Collingsworth. On April 24, 1829, Van Buren responded to Jackson:

> I shall cheerfully do what you may desire in regard to the appointment in Nashville but as I have not the slightest choice between the Candidates and no personal knowledge of either of them save Mr. Balch and that very superficially, I should be in no small degree embarrassed in the execution of a trust you have in so kind and flattering a manner committed to me.

On April 30, 1829, Van Buren directed that James Collingsworth be appointed as district attorney.[95]

Though they both passed him over for United States Attorney in 1829, Jackson and Van Buren would eventually do right by Balch. In 1836, during President Jackson's administration, Balch was appointed to a Commission, which had been created July 1, 1836, to investigate the alleged frauds committed on the Creek Indians in the sales of their reservations. Balch and his colleagues received their instructions from the War Department on July 12, 1836, and would submit their 101 page report on July 3, 1838.[96]

In 1840, Van Buren would appoint Balch as United States District Judge for the middle district of Florida.[97] Balch would remain on the bench for just over a year before resigning. Balch's time in Florida was during a time of unrest when various Native American tribes joined with the Seminoles in fighting what is known as the Second Seminole War.[98] It was a time of political conflict as well. Balch wrote President Van Buren explaining that "the condition of affairs in this territory is deplorable," and that "the leading men are

---

95. The Papers of Andrew Jackson, Volume VII, 1829. University of Tennessee Press, Knoxville TN, 2007: 181-182.

96. Message from the President of the United States Transmitting Information in relation to Alleged Frauds on the Creek Indian in the Sale of their Reservations. House of Representatives, Executive Doc. No. 452. 25th Congress, Second Session. July 3, 1838: 1-2.

97. Manley at 84 and Balch at 207.

98. Manley at 84.

divided into bitter parties and violence is the order of the day." In his resignation letter to President John Tyler, Balch cited "excess labor in the discharge of official duties as Judge of the U[nited] states of America for the District of Middle Florida" as having made him susceptible to a fever he had acquired. He apparently had sought medical care in New York and was treated with rest in Newport, Rhode Island before he resigned on August 5, 1841. He returned to the private practice of law in Nashville in 1842.

Balch died in Nashville on June 21, 1853.[99]

---

99. Ibid, 185.

3

The Magness Family

Jonathan Magness and his family were pioneers in Tennessee during the first decade of the nineteenth century. They arrived sometime before the summer of 1806 seeking a new life and distance from a troublesome family in North Carolina and Kentucky. In just a few short years, they would clash with the establishment in Tennessee and find troubles of their own.

The father of Jonathan Magness, Peregrine Magness Jr., was born in colonial Prince George's County, Maryland around 1722.[1] His father, Peregrine Sr., was a blacksmith and is recorded in the Prince George's County, Maryland, deed books as early as 1729.[2] He

---

1. Thomas G. Webb, *The Webb Families of DeKalb County, Tennessee and 23 Related Families*. Smithville, TN: Bradley Printing Company, 2002, 226. Thomas Webb provides a well-researched and documented history of the Magness family.

2. Prince George's County, Maryland, Deed Book Q, 218.

remained there and is listed in the county deed books in 1732, 1751, 1752 and 1753.[3] By July 16, 1765, Peregrine Sr. was living in Fairfax County, Virginia, where he voted for Colonel George Washington and Colonel John West for the House of Burgesses.[4]

Peregrine Sr. prospered in his blacksmith trade and owned land, slaves, and livestock.[5] On April 22, 1757, he gave to his son "Perygrine Mackaness Junior" (because of the "natural love and affection" he felt toward him) one half of a tract of 105 acres called Part of Stoke, lying in Prince George's Peregrine Sr. County, Maryland. Mary, the wife of Peregrine Sr. and mother of Peregrine Jr., also released any claims she had to the property.[6]

Peregrine Magness Jr. had at least two siblings: Samuel and a sister who married and had a son named Thomas Gaines.[7] By the time his father gave him land in 1757, Peregrine Jr. had been married to a woman named Mary (like his mother) for about twelve years and had five sons.[8] Many old histories and genealogies of Peregrine Jr. opine that his wife's name was Sarah Hamrick. However, in the words of historian Thomas Webb, "all the evidence indicates that she was definitely *not* Sarah Hamrick."[9] While her maiden is unknown, Peregrine's will gives the best evidence that her name was Mary. She was the mother of Jonathan, the fifth son, who was born in 1756.[10]

About three years later, Peregrine Jr. began moving his family west. He sold 51 acres of the land his father had given him to a man named George Naylor for 20 pounds on February 9, 1760. That same day, his wife Mary relinquished her right of dower to the land.[11]

---

3. Webb, *The Webb Families of DeKalb County*, 226–228. See also V. L. Skinner, "Abstracts of the Prerogative Court of Maryland."

4. Thomas G. Webb, *Early Virginia Families with Tennessee Connections*. Smithville, TN: Bradley Printing Company, 2009, 299.

5. Webb, *The Webb Families of DeKalb County*, 228.

6. Prince George's County, Maryland, Deed Book NN, 522.

7. Webb, *Early Virginia Families*, 299.

8. Webb, *The Webb Families of DeKalb County*, 229.

9. *Ibid.*

10. *Ibid*, 232.

11. Prince George's County, Maryland, Deed Book RR, 44.

Peregrine Jr. was recorded in Bedford County, Virginia in 1765.[12] He was ordered to "help view" a new road that ran from the ferry of Nicholas Davis to James Callaway's road. It appears to have been near his home.[13] At that time, Bedford County extended farther south than it does today and was one county north of North Carolina.

By 1768, Peregrine Magness Jr. was in Mecklenburg County, North Carolina. An order was made on December 21 to survey 200 acres on both sides of Knob Creek in that county for his benefit.[14] A month later, on January 23, 1769, he bought 300 acres on Buffalo Creek in Tryon County from William Sims.[15] Tryon County was created in 1768 from the part of Mecklenburg County west of the Catawba River.[16] Peregrine Jr. continued to acquire land. He entered for the record 300 acres on both sides of Hickory Creek in November 1769. By 1795, he was the owner of more than 1,500 acres in Tryon County, which later became Rutherford, Lincoln, and Cleveland counties.[17]

In April 1770, the Tryon County Court minutes recorded that Peregrine Jr. was commissioned as an ensign in the county militia.[18] When the Tryon Committee of Safety was organized on July 26, 1775, it included "Captain Mackness' Company."[19] This committee would draft a resolution calling for the redress of grievances inflicted upon the colonies by the British Parliament and King George III. These so-called "Tryon Resolves" were among the earliest declarations of their sort and predated the Declaration of In-

---

12. Bedford County, Virginia, Court Order Book 3 (February 1765), 172.
13. Webb, *The Webb Families of DeKalb County*, 230.
14. *Ibid.*
15. Tryon County, North Carolina, Deed Book, 1, 51.
16. Clarence W. Griffin, *History of Old Tryon and Rutherford Counties, North Carolina, 1730-1936*. Asheville, NC: Miller Printing Company, 1937, 7.
17. Webb, *The Webb Families of DeKalb County, Tennessee*, 230.
18. Griffin, *History of Old Tryon and Rutherford Counties*, 10. Webb, *The Webb Families of DeKalb County, Tennessee*, 230.
19. *Minutes of the Tryon County Committee of Safety, Tryon County (N.C.). Committee of Safety, January 23, 1776 - January 24, 1776*. Colonial and State Records of North Carolina, Volume 10, 423–424.

dependence by almost a year.[20] "Perrygreen Mackness" Jr. joined his colleagues in signing the Tryon Resolves on August 14, 1775.[21]

Peregrine's three oldest sons, William, James, and Peregrine III (although he is also referred to as "Jr."), all appear to have served in the Revolution. William was a Captain in Colonel William Graham's Tryon Regiment of Militia in February and March of 1776.[22] James may have been killed at the Battle of Cowpens on January 17, 1781, though the record is spotty and incomplete.[23] Peregrine III ("Jr.") enlisted in Captain Eli Kershaw's Company of Colonel Thomson's Regiment of South Carolina Rangers.[24]

After the war, Peregrine Magness Jr. prospered. The tax rolls show that his wealth increased and his children were establishing themselves around him.[25] His oldest son William began to acquire land in 1774 and would possess some 2,500 acres by the time of his death in 1816.[26] In 1779, Peregrine's fifth son, Jonathan Magness, was granted 150 acres on Big Hickory Creek in Tryon County, joining the land of his father. This property was later sold in 1790 when he bought 300 acres on Brushy Creek in Rutherford County two years earlier. He owned some five other tracts of land as well.[27]

While things were going well for the older Magnesses in North Carolina, the younger children of Peregrine Jr. would soon get in trouble with the law and ultimately bring ruin upon their father. Jonathan Magness would watch as the actions of his brothers exposed the entire family to financial woes and drive many of them

---

20. Griffin, *History of Old Tryon and Rutherford Counties*, 17–18.

21. *Minutes of the Tryon County Committee of Safety, August 14, 1775.* Colonial and State Records of North Carolina, Volume 10, 162.

22. *Roster of Soldiers from North Carolina in the American Revolution.* Durham NC: North Carolina Daughters of the American Revolution, 1932, 42.

23. Webb, *The Webb Families of DeKalb County, Tennessee*, 232.

24. "Papers of the First Council of Safety of the Revolutionary Party in South Carolina, June-November, 1775." *The South Carolina Historical and Genealogical Magazine.* Vol. I, Number 2 (April, 1900), 120.

25. Webb, *The Webb Families of DeKalb County, Tennessee*, 230.

26. *Ibid*, 231.

27. *Ibid*, 233.

out of the state. Thoughts of these days must have lingered in Jonathan's mind when he found trouble himself in Tennessee.

Peregrine Jr's eighth son, Joseph, married Arabella Twitty in 1787. Peregrine Jr's sixth son, Zachariah, was accused of raping Arabella in 1789 and "she accused Joseph of aiding and abetting in the act."[28] Peregrine Jr. posted 250 pounds as security for Zachariah's appearance in court. Jonathan posted 200 pounds as security for the appearance of Joseph.[29] Zachariah apparently fled the jurisdiction to avoid the trial and left his father in debt to Rutherford County. It seems Joseph was not convicted of aiding and abetting in the rape of his wife, but he was in and out of Rutherford County's court for various matters—including a divorce—through 1794. By 1795, he had left the area and moved to Woodford County, Kentucky.[30]

George Magness, the tenth and youngest son of Peregrine Jr., was in trouble with the law from an early age. Between 1794 and 1795, he was involved in several legal dramas in North Carolina. He was convicted of petty larceny in Lincoln County in April 1794 and sentenced to "receive ten lashes on his bare back well laid." Meanwhile, for some unknown reason, Polly Durham sued him in Rutherford County. The suit was dismissed in April, but by October 1784, his brother Jonathan posted a two hundred pound bond on behalf of George Magness to indemnify Rutherford County from providing maintenance for the "base born child" that had been delivered by Polly Durham.[31] In 1795, George was accused of horse theft in Burke County. Though he was found not guilty, he was ordered to pay court costs. He was unable to pay and was held in jail from June 26, 1795, until September 16, 1795. At some point he married Polly Durham who gave him a legitimate heir named Perrygreen Magness on May 23, 1796.[32]

---

28. *Ibid*, 230.
29. *Ibid*, 241.
30. *Ibid*, 239.
31. *Ibid*, 236.

32. *Ibid*, 242. This Perrygreen Magness is often confused with his cousin of the same name, the son of Jonathan Magness. John B. Cowden makes this mistake in his otherwise well-documented book about the Magness trial, *Tennessee's Celebrated Case "Causa Celebre."*

Not to be outdone, Peregrine Jr's ninth son, Robert, was also involved with the law. He was accused of stealing "a bay horse with a blaze face" in January 1793. According to Jeanette Stubblefield, who possessed a copy of that particular court case, the arrest arose from an agreement Robert had with another man to swap horses. Each man was supposed to take the other's horse and keep it for ten days to determine if they truly wanted to make the trade. Before the ten days were over, Robert decided that he did not want to make the exchange and proceeded to return the horse he had borrowed. The other man refused to give Robert his horse back. Robert then broke the lock on the man's stable door, removed his own horse, and left. The man brought charges against Robert for "stealing" his horse.[33]

Robert Magness was acquitted of the theft, but later was convicted of perjury. He fled North Carolina, resulting in the forfeiture of his bond and leaving his father and his brother Jonathan to pay it. Over the next score of years, Robert could be found in Tennessee, the Indiana Territory, back to Tennessee, and Arkansas.

In arrears to the county for the bonds of their relatives, Peregrine and Jonathan Magness had to liquidate their holdings. William and Benjamin Magness bought what property they could from their father and brother, but in the summer of 1796, the sheriff sold ten tracts of land in Rutherford County belonging to either Peregrine or Jonathan Magness.[34] More than 1,150 acres of Peregrine's land was sold at the Sheriff's auction.[35]

Peregrine Magness Jr. left North Carolina about this time and went to Warren County, Kentucky, where his son Joseph had settled. By the time Peregrine Jr. died in Bowling Green, Kentucky, in July 1800, George and Joseph were living in Warren County, Kentucky.[36]

Jonathan Magness moved south of Warren County with his family to nearby Tennessee. His son Morgan was born at the Hermitage in eastern Davidson County in December 1796.[37] Jonathan

---

33. Webb, *The Webb Families of DeKalb County*, 241.
34. *Ibid*, 235.
35. *Ibid*, 231.
36. *Ibid*.
37. *Arkansas Gazette*, September 16, 1871, page 1, column C.

was well settled in western Wilson County, Tennessee, by August 24, 1806, when he paid $800 for 640 acres near Stones River and the Davidson County line.[38] Witnesses to this purchase were his sons Perrygreen and John. On September 3, 1807, Jonathan paid $640 for another 640-acre tract on Stuart's Creek in Wilson County with his sons John and David Magness being witnesses to the purchase.[39] Jonathan was assigned the military land grant of John Ranier for 340 acres in Wilson County, including the "Jordin Reaves improvement," on April 7, 1809.[40]

With his move to the Tennessee frontier, Jonathan Magness probably hoped to flee from the woes and reputation of his brothers. But it only put him in proximity to the violent men and atmosphere that would lead him and his sons David and Perrygreen to their own troubles with the law. According to one history, from 1782 to 1804, Tennessee was a "bloody ground", with the Lindsay, Fletcher, Lafferty, and Magness families always in the "thickest of the fight."[41] The fighting these families did on the frontier was savage as evidenced by three different Fletchers and two members of the Lafferty family being "scalped in cold blood."[42] It was in this feral environment that the tough-minded and obstinate Magnesses would get in the fight of their lives.

---

38. Wilson County, Tennessee. Deed Book B, 227.
39. Wilson County, Tennessee, Deed Book C, 113.
40. Early Tennessee General Land Grants. Roll 28, Book D, recorded March 19, 1811, Nashville, TN: Tennessee State Library and Archives.
41. Josiah H. Shinn, *Pioneers and Makers of Arkansas*. Washington, D.C.: Genealogical and Historical Publishing Company, 1908, 346.
42. *Ibid.*

4

Tennessee v. David Magness: The First Trial Begins

The trial of the Magnesses was set to begin on November 12, 1810. Trials in those days were great entertainment for the masses.[1] People traveled from miles around to witness the battles between the lawyers of the day and the Magness trial would showcase the greatest lawyers of the old Southwest. Little existed in the way of entertainment on the frontier and a murder trial certainly made for high drama and great entertainment.

The Magness trial was an uproarious affair in its time. In his 1879 biography of Andrew Jackson, historian James Parton wrote:

---

1. Heller, *Democracy's Lawyer*, 2.

> ...no Tennessean, who can remember as far back as 1810, can have forgotten the killing of Patton Anderson, and the exciting trial of the murderers.²

Citing a lawyer who was present, Parton wrote that the trial was attended by a "great concourse of people" and General Jackson himself attended.³

With the coming trial, the small town of Franklin, Tennessee, was occupied by two camps. One of the town's two taverns was occupied by Jackson and the Anderson party, and the other by the supporters of the Magnesses.⁴ It is not hard to imagine how passions for the case might be on display and tensions could rise where two camps of armed men drank and stewed with resentment in close proximity to each other. At one point, Jackson, apparently drunk, addressed his partisans from the piazza of the tavern he occupied. During this address, some member of the Magness group walked by, shrugged his shoulders, and mocked Jackson with an audible "*Pshaw!*" Jackson then stopped his speech to find the transgressor in the crowd, shouting, "Who dares to say *pshaw* at me? By (God)! I'll knock any man's head off who says *pshaw* at me!"⁵

The culprit continued his saunter, presumably under the glare of Jackson, who went about finishing his speech.⁶⁷

---

2. James Parton, *Life of Andrew Jackson in Three Volumes*. Vol. 1, 342.

3. Benton, 736.

4. Parton, 342.

5. *Ibid*.

6. *Ibid*, 344.

7. In his 1933 biography *Andrew Jackson: The Border Captain*, Marquis James retells the story of Jackson's after-dinner tirade and cites Parton as his source. He suggests that Parton's "informant" was likely a man named W.B. Lewis or someone else close to Jackson. James explains: "Jackson's great interest in this trial is attested by the fact that after his death between fifty and sixty pages of manuscript bearing on it were found among his papers. They are now in the Jackson Papers, Library of Congress, in a folder marked 'Doubtful and Undated'." These papers (not in Jackson's handwriting) were eventually determined to be the notes of Jackson's friend, aide-de-camp, and biographer John Reid. The Library of Congress now catalogues these notes in a file that accompanies three bound volumes of Reid's other manuscripts. I have numbered the pages in the order they were found in the folder, but because they are not bound, the numbering is not reliable.

At the opening of the trial, Judge Stuart made the decision to bifurcate (or separate) the cases and try David first. According to notes of the case:

> In this case David Magness the principal, and Perigrine Magness and Jonathon Magness accessories. An application was made by the Council for the prisoners to bring on the trial of Perigrine before that of David founded upon an affidavit of David and Jonathon stating that if Perigrine should be acquitted his evidence would be of material service in the trial of David. After a learned argument by council on both sides the Judge expresses the opinion that the trial of the principal should in this case be introduced first.[8]

A jury of "good and lawful men" of Williamson County, consisting of Henry Cook, James Gideon, James Hicks, Samuel McCutchen, Reuben Parks, Andrew Goff, Robert McLeland, Thomas Ridley, James Hartgrove, Richard Puckett, Thomas Berry, and Thomas Walker was impaneled to hear the case.[9] Constables were assigned to care for the jury and are mentioned throughout the court documents as they received orders from the court. They were Caleb Manley, Kemp Holland, John L. Fielder, and Peter Reeves.[10]

In order to convict David Magness of murder, the prosecution would have to prove each element of the crime, including "malice aforethought." In order to convict Jonathan and Perrygreen Magness, the prosecution had to prove that they were in a conspiracy with David to kill Anderson and that they aided in the planning of the killing. To convict all three, they needed to prove the Magnesses had contemplated and premeditated the killing of Patton Anderson. To prove conspiracy, the prosecution would need to show that there was intent to form an agreement to commit an unlawful act. The defense was not going to contest that David Magness had shot Anderson. Instead, they were seeking an affirmative defense

---

8. Reid, 98.
9. *Williamson County, Tennessee, Miscellaneous Records*, Volume 1, 95–96.
10. *Ibid*, 125, 105, 108, 104.

to the crime of murder in that David Magness was seeking to prevent Anderson from killing his father. The key issue for the defense team in proving this defense-of-others argument would be that it was reasonable for David Magness to believe Patton Anderson was posing an imminent danger of grave harm on Jonathan Magness when he shot him.

The attorneys in the case argued at length about the elements of the crimes, the defenses, and the standards that should be applied by the jury. At trial, the attorneys on both sides would call witnesses who could bolster their opposing theories of the case. Ultimately, the prosecution would focus on old grievances that the Magnesses had with Patton Anderson. They would call witnesses who offered testimony to show premeditation and deliberation prior to the actual shooting. The defense would bring witnesses who would testify that they believed Jonathan Magness was being threatened with imminent harm at which time his son stepped in to shoot Anderson.

In his summation, Felix Grundy described the situation from the perspective of his clients, the defendants:

> The prisoner, his father and brother, on their way to the Muscle Shoals had occasion to call at Shelbyville where the circuit court was in session, on business. Anderson was also there. On Wednesday, Anderson, with Drake, and the prosecutor went into the house of Newsom for the purpose of taking a drink of grog. Jonathan Magness, the father, about the same time had entered the house for the same purpose, but perceiving Anderson, and knowing that his heart had long been full of bitterness toward him, he retires to the distant part of the room that he might be entirely out of his way; and there enters into a peaceable conversation with Drake.

Grundy continued:

> Anderson follows him up in order to insult him—which he presently does in the most offensive manner. The old man, who though disposed to peace, was no coward, repels the insult, in terms as warm, though not so bitter, as those in which it had

been offered. The prisoner who just then was making ready to set out on his journey, hears the noise, and enters the room with his saddle bags and holsters on his arm. Quietly he takes a seat on the opposite side, in hopes that the quarrel might blow over without any dangerous consequences. But his hopes were doomed to disappointment. The quarrel, warm at first, instantly becomes violent. Anderson in a paroxysm of rage draws a dirk from his side—swears he will kill—and raises the hand which grasped it, to execute the threat.[11]

The Testimony

The prosecution led with witnesses who suggested that there was an old grievance between the Magnesses and Anderson and that this grievance led the Magnesses to conspire to kill Anderson. The nature of the grievance was centered on a trade in horses. According to the prosecution's line of thought, a man named Riggs had told Anderson that he had land to sell. Anderson bought a warrant for the land for the price of $2,500 in the form of several horses that were delivered ten days after the agreement.[12] The land warrant turned out to be a forgery. Sometime after this was discovered, a man named Eskridge, who had served as an agent for Riggs, "comes to Anderson riding a particular horse" that appeared to have been in the lot traded to Riggs. Anderson inquired as to what had become of his property after the warrant was determined to be counterfeit. He was told that "Jim R. and Old Magness" were involved the scheme." Anderson went out with a group of men to confront Magness.

Anderson and his men found some of the horses that he had traded with Riggs at the home of Jonathan Magness. Anderson confronted Magness, claiming the horses were his, pointing out that one of them was being ridden by the very man who had cheated him out of them. Magness explained that Riggs had left the horses there for care and feeding and would be compensated with a few of the horses. Magness told Anderson to take the horses if they

---

11. Reid, 64.
12. *Ibid*, 167.

were in fact his but that he expected Anderson to pay for the care and feeding they had already provided.[13] Anderson became angry, accused the Magnesses of stealing the horses, and threatened Jonathan Magness with his life.[14] Anderson then took at least one horse that the Magnesses claimed to be theirs, but refused to pay for it, telling them, "if your right is better than mine, prove it and get your horse."[15]

The Magnesses hoped to be compensated for the care they had provided and for the horses taken from them. Anderson, for his part, filed suit in Bedford County against Riggs.[16] Anderson traveled to Shelbyville to attend the hearing and press his case in a trial that was scheduled for October 24, 1810—the very day he would be shot.[17] While historians such as Parton suggest that it was the Magnesses themselves who were being sued by Anderson, the trial documents indicate otherwise.[18] Jonathan Magness did assert that he was in Shelbyville the day of the shooting because he expected to collect money that day, presumably after the suit between Riggs and Anderson was settled.[19]

As the murder trial continued, the prosecution called John Casey to the witness stand.[20] Casey testified that the day before Anderson was killed, he saw the Magnesses at Shelbyville who told him there was a dispute about horses. David and Jonathan told Casey that

---

13. *Ibid*, 167.

14. Gary Alan Webb, "The Magness Trials." Williamson County Historical Society, Volume 15 (1984), 23.

15. Testimony of Thomas Mitchel and John McPeak, Trial Notes of John Reid, John Reid Papers, 1802–1842, Library of Congress MMC-3365, 11. (Hereafter referred to as Reid trial notes.)

16. Webb, "The Magness Trials."

17. *Ibid*.

18. Reid trial notes, 24–25. One of the items listed by prosecutors as a "display of the guilt of the prisoner" was "going to Bedford County without necessity when he was certain of meeting Anderson there."

19. Louis Gillespie Lynch, compiler, Williamson County, Tennessee, Miscellaneous Records, Volume 3, 1980, 54. Affidavit of Jonathan Magness.

20. The testimony of John Casey is found in pages 1 and 116 of the Reid trial notes in the order of the file. It is possible that one set of notes is from the trial of David and the other from the trial of Jonathan. Because the notes are sworn testimony and corroborative, I have used them collectively in describing Casey's testimony.

Anderson had two of their horses—a sorrel stud and a bay stud colt. The Magnesses asked Casey speak to Anderson on the subject in order to get him to pay them some sort of satisfaction for the horses. Casey said that J. Riggs had given the horses to the Magnesses.

Casey testified that he spoke with Anderson who, in turn, said he owed the Magnesses nothing. He stated that Anderson said the Magnesses were "bad men" and he wished to have nothing to do with them. If he did owe them anything, they would have to sue him to get the money. Casey then testified that he saw David and Jonathan afterward and informed them that Anderson would have nothing to do with them. Casey said he observed that they were "sorry for it; that they wished the thing settled." When asked about how the Magnesses had come to possess the horses in the dispute, Casey replied that Jonathan Magness had been keeping horses that belonged to Riggs, but when Anderson came to take Riggs' horses, he took away two of them. Anderson claimed that one of these horses he took, the bay horse, was the horse that "Riggs was riding when he had cheated him."[21]

Casey further testified that on the day of the killing, he saw Anderson at the courthouse. He claimed Anderson told him that he was going to the house of William Newsom to meet Isaac Williams to conduct a trade for some African American slaves. Anderson and Williams drank together and discussed their trade. Casey then testified that soon after, Perrygreen Magness came into Newsom's house. He spoke to Casey and left. He came back with Jonathan, David, and Jordan Reaves. Casey said that David sat on a bench and that he observed Jonathan in a conversation with Drake. Anderson got up and asked if Drake and Jonathan were talking about J. Riggs. If so, Drake need not listen to Jonathan because he wouldn't be telling the truth. Anderson told Drake not to talk with "that old villain," to which Jonathan "reproachfully" told Anderson "to go off—that he wished to have nothing to do with him." Then Anderson raised his arm to strike Magness, but Drake somehow got in the way and Anderson "drew his dirk." Casey testified that he took Anderson by the arms and "shoved him back about 9 feet," then the pistol was

---

21. Reid trial notes, 117.

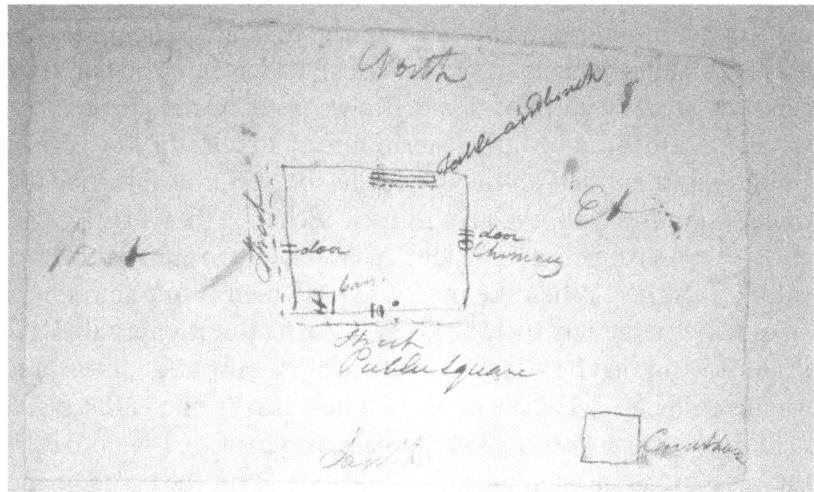

Diagram of the murder scene from the notes of John Reid

fired. He stated that he was "certain Anderson did not resist as he shoved him back."[22]

William Rogers testified that he was within two feet of Anderson when the pistol cracked and was looking at him. He said that Anderson did not claim that he would kill the "damned old rascal" and saw "no more reason for killing Anderson than there is for Newsom to shoot him." Rogers stated that Casey held Anderson before him when he shoved him back and he did not see an attempt by Anderson to shove forward as if to strike. Rogers thought Casey let Anderson go and was certain that Anderson did not attempt to shove forward. He testified Casey moved a little and Anderson might have moved as far, but did not go forward.[23]

This point in the action was the critical moment for the jury. The fate of David Magness would be decided on whether the jurors believed it was reasonable for David Magness to think his father was about to suffer harm at the hands of Anderson. The alternative, the other theory, was that of a premeditated shooting.

Stephen Bedford testified for the prosecution that about 15 minutes before the pistol fired, he saw David Magness sitting on the

---

22. *Ibid*, 1.
23. *Ibid*, 18.

bench with his holster on his left arm and his right hand under the holster. Alluding to premeditation, he claimed that he could not "conceive a more favorable position to draw a pistol instantaneously."

Benjamin Bradford, the sheriff and tax collector of Bedford County, testified that on the day Anderson was killed, he saw the three Magnesses with several other men, including the two Eskridges and Reeves, sitting on a log below Newsom's tavern apparently consulting together. When the men saw Anderson riding into town, all quickly "jerked up their heads as if alarmed at his appearance." Bradford said that he was between the courthouse and some stores when a pistol fired. He saw David Magness run by him with a pistol in his hand and holsters and saddle bags over his arm. Bradford took the pistols from him and identified the pistols for the jury. During questioning, the sheriff stated that David Magness never claimed to have killed Anderson in defense of his father.[24]

Edward Ward testified that he saw Casey shove Anderson back nine feet when the pistol fired and David Magness immediately ran. Ward was positive that Jonathan Magness could have gotten away safely when Anderson was shoved back. He didn't believe Jonathan Magness was in danger even if Anderson could have rushed over Casey who was holding him back.[25]

Mal Gilchrist testified that he saw Anderson with the dirk in his left hand. He saw Casey take Anderson by the arms and shove him below the door and that Anderson was not resisting him. He further testified that Jonathan Magness walked to the chimney and looked into the middle of the house. At that point, Gilchrist saw David Magness advance and fire on Anderson as Casey shoved him. Gilchrist claimed that Jonathan Magness was twelve or fourteen feet from Anderson and retreating when David advanced.[26]

John Drake testified that he left the courthouse with Anderson to go to Newsom's to conclude a trade with Williams about slaves. There he witnessed Anderson raise his left hand to strike Jonathan Magness. Jonathan put his hand into his pocket, as if to draw a knife,

24. Ibid, 2.
25. Ibid, 1.
26. Ibid, 2.

and at that point Anderson drew his dirk and held it in his left hand. Drake stated that Casey took hold of Anderson and shoved him, at which point Jonathan Magness went back towards the chimney. David Magness advanced from the bench, came within three feet of Anderson, fired the pistol, and fled. Drake testified that he believed Anderson never saw David until the pistol fired. Drake questioned David after the shooting as to why he killed Anderson and David "gave no satisfactory answer." Drake added that David gave no pretense of having taken his action to save or protect his father.

Upon cross-examination, Drake testified that while the Magnesses were in confinement (at the Stone house) on Saturday, David offered to shake hands with him but Drake refused his hand. "I am not so much to blame as another in this room," he told Drake, which Drake took to mean David's father, Jonathan.[27] This statement was key to the prosecution's theory that there was a conspiracy to kill Anderson. In his closing, Jenkin Whiteside described Magness as attempting to apologize to Drake for his conduct. Whiteside argued that it was the wish of David Magness to convince Drake that his father's influence had prompted him to kill his friend.

William Tune testified that he was passing by and saw Perrygreen and David Magness going to Newsom's. He saw Perrygreen stop David and ask if his pistol was in order. According to Tune, Perrygreen adjusted David's pistols for him. He drew up the right hand pistol as high as the lock, then let it down and turned the butt end around so that it could be conveniently taken hold of by David's right hand. Tune's testimony was damaging to the defense in that it could infer some level of force was being premeditated by the Magnesses. The defense counsel attacked the character of Tune and portrayed him as a man "of loose and immoral habits, addicted to drunkenness and gambling with no character to lose." The defense said of Tune, "[H]e is little solicitous about public opinion, which is the only thing to keep a man within in proper bounds where virtue is wanting." Defense counsel then posed the following to the jury:

---

27. *Ibid*, 2, 4.

> Is this the man, gentlemen, who is to swear away the lives of your fellow men! Are the property and lives of the most worthy among us to be at the disposal of such men!! Wretched is that country where such witnesses are received—doubly wretched where their evidence is accredited!

Dr. Samuel Hogg was called as a character witness to support William Tune. He stated that he had known Tune for five or six years and considered him to be "an honest and true man." Dr. Hogg "would believe him on his oath."[28] Lemuel Hutchins was also called to support Tune and testified that he had known him to be an honest man who supported his mother and himself by his labor.[29] John H. Eaton testified he had known Tune in North Carolina and that he "supported great character."[30]

John Griffin was next called to the stand to testify. He met David Magness on the Wednesday morning before the shooting. He told David that he had "an excellent pair of pistols" and David asked if he could borrow them. Griffin testified that David intended "to take horses to the range" and to go to the Muscle Shoals and for that reason only needed Griffin's pistols.[31] David told him he would be back in three weeks. Griffin refused to loan David the pistols unless he would return them; if they were not returned, he would be paid with a horse worth fifty dollars.[32] Griffin stated that on Friday night, he stayed at Broadways with David, Perrygreen, and other men. The group started out Sunday morning from Jonathan Magness' home. Griffin observed the butt of a "horseman's pistol" in Jonathan Magness's saddle bags and heard him ask a man named Wright if he had the bullets. When Wright replied that he didn't, Jonathan told Perrygreen to go back and get them. Griffin said that David went by

28. *Ibid*, 21.
29. *Ibid*.
30. *Ibid*.
31. Lynch, comp., Williamson County, Tennessee, Miscellaneous Records, Volume 3, 51.
32. Reid trial notes, 6.

his house to retrieve pistols and powder but that David never spoke to him about the pistols while in the company of others.[33]

Griffin believed the Magnesses were in Shelbyville the day of the shooting because Jonathan Magness apparently expected to receive some money there on that day. Griffin believed that David Magness intended to go on to Muscle Shoals and for that purpose had brought his pistols.[34] Upon hearing that Patton Anderson was killed by David, he was afraid the act had been committed with his pistol. Upon cross examination, Griffin stated he thought it was otherwise normal for David to take horses to the Duck River (which runs through Shelbyville) to winter, but he never knew David or Jonathan Magness to carry pistols before.[35]

Whiteside brought this testimony into light by arguing:

> No man ever prepared himself with more deliberation and caution for the destruction of a fellow being. He had at an extravagant price, furnished himself with the best brace of pistols which the country could afford—prepared balls,—and obtained a gourd of the best powder. Now I ask if all these warlike arrangements were made to resist a danger which he apprehended. Did he believe that Anderson would assail him? Why then was he never heard—when travelling thus accoutered, or when at Shelbyville—to express his fears! Did he tell Griffin when he borrowed the pistols that he apprehended danger from Anderson? Did he avow that as his motive for borrowing them? Did he to any human being ever explain his reason for this warlike array?![36]

The defense called witnesses who described Patton Anderson as a man to be feared. Defense witnesses suggested that the Magnesses should have been reasonably afraid for the life of Jonathan Magness

---

33. *Ibid*, 6.
34. Lynch, 51.
35. Reid trial notes, 6.
36. *Ibid*, 67.

and defense counsel capitalized on Anderson's reputation for anger and drunkenness.

Men who had run-ins with Anderson were called by the defense. A man named Hall, who admitted there was "violent personal enmity between himself and Anderson," testified that Anderson was a "mighty rash man when intoxicated" and a "man of violent passion."[37] Joel Lewis, who had "enmity" with Patton Anderson's brother, William P. Anderson (but not with Anderson himself), described Patton Anderson as a "dangerous man" who carried arms.[38] An individual identified as Doctor Kavanaugh also described Anderson as a "dangerous man" who "carried arms" and explained that there had been enmity between his son-in-law and Patton Anderson.[39]

James Gilbert testified that two hours before the incident, he rode his horse into the company of men that included Anderson. Anderson observed that Gilbert's horse was a fine mare and asked whether or not Gilbert came across it honestly. Anderson commented that there were some other rogues and rascals in the vicinity. He noticed the Magnesses and stated he intended to kill some of them even at the risk of his own life. Gilbert also called into question the testimony of the tailor, Mr. Tune, and offered that Mr. Tune could not have been at William Newsom's house at the time he swore that Perrygreen Magness went into the Newsom house in the company of David Magness. He testified that Tune had been, then and for some time, at a house some distance away engaged in raffling.[40]

Nat. Williams testified that he was also raffling for shoes when Anderson was killed and that Tune was with them. He believed Anderson to be "of dangerous character."[41] Gideon Harman testified that he was engaged in a raffle for a half hour before the pistol fired and that Tune was either there or came in immediately. He stated that those involved could not have been engaged in the raf-

---

37. *Ibid*, 13.
38. *Ibid*, 14.
39. *Ibid*.
40. Lynch, comp., Williamson County, Tennessee Miscellaneous Records, Volume 3. Reid trial notes, 17.
41. Reid trial notes, 13.

fle for more than three-quarters of an hour.[42] John Saddler testified that he was engaged in raffling with Tune about an hour before the pistol fired and was in partnership in the raffle.[43] Saddler then confirmed where he lived on cross-examination but could not answer when asked this salacious question: "Did you ever bite off Dick Scrugg's nose?"[44]

Archibald Simpson was called and testified that Drake and Jonathan Magness were in conversation together when Anderson approached. Alluding to Jonathan, Anderson said that "no rascal who had been arraigned for cow-stealing should stand in his presence or he would kill him." Simpson stated that Jonathan Magness informed Anderson that if he did, it was at the risk of his own life. Anderson then repeated his threat and immediately drew his knife. Just as Anderson had the dirk raised to stab Jonathan Magness, the pistol fired. Simpson testified that at the time of the gunshot, Anderson was "a step or so" from Jonathan Magness who was himself "within a foot or two" of the door. [45]

The defense called Jordan Reeves to the stand to refute the prosecution's assertion that Jonathan Magness was in no danger. Reeves was the brother-in-law of the defendant. He testified that Jonathan was in imminent danger when Anderson was shot. Reeves said that Anderson was not more than four feet from Jonathan Magness and had his hand up with the dirk in his hand. Anderson stood toward Jonathan with an "attitude that it was to be expected that in an instant the dirk would have been plunged to his heart."[46]

Matthew S. Montgomery testified that he heard loud talk where Jonathan Magness was standing and heard Magness exclaim, "If you lay your hands upon me, it will be at your own risk." He saw Anderson pull his dirk before somebody caught Anderson by the arms above the elbow and shoved him back." Montgomery observed David Magness standing up towards the east door, with saddlebags

42. *Ibid*, 16.
43. *Ibid*, 17.
44. *Ibid*.
45. Lynch, comp., *Williamson County, Tennessee Miscellaneous Records*, Volume 3. Affidavit of Jonathan Magness.
46. Reid trial notes, 28, 39.

on his left arm, and a bear skin under them. He believed Magness had the pistols under the saddle bags. At this point, Montgomery "jumped out the door" for his own safety. He had gone eight or ten feet when he heard the pistol fire.[47]

Hugh Barnett testified that at the time of the altercation, he was standing "close to them, and could distinctly see and understand what took place between the said parties." He believed the assault was an "inevitable necessity" of delivering a fatal blow to save Jonathan Magness' life, which had been threatened and violently assaulted by Patton Anderson.[48] He saw some persons "jerk" Anderson down and that he heard Anderson twice say he would kill the "old rascal."[49] Barnett testified that as the word escaped from his mouth a second time, the pistol cracked. At the time of the gunshot, Anderson might have been on Jonathan Magness "at a shingle dash" had he not been "held by an arm sufficiently strong to intercept his fury."[50] The prosecution then called Edward Cage and Nicholas Nall as rebuttal witnesses to Barnett. Cage testified that he saw Hugh Barnett at a place or home called "Sharpes" and heard Barnett say he was not in the house when the pistol fired. Instead, he had stepped out and when he came back, Anderson was lying dead.[51] Nall corroborated Cage's testimony.[52]

Lewis Newsom (Old Newsom) stated that he had sat upon the log at the Newsom House in conversation with Magness "when one said there is Patton Anderson now."[53] Newsom observed Anderson say that he wanted to kill Jonathan Magness. Alluding to Magness, Anderson said he would kill "all horse thieves, cow thieves, hog thieves" and he spoke so loudly that every person in the house might hear it. Newsom also noted that Anderson had been seen in

---

47. *Ibid*, 19.

48. Lynch, comp., *Williamson County, Tennessee Miscellaneous Records*, Volume 3. Affidavit of Jonathan Magness.

49. Reid trial notes, 9.

50. Lynch, comp., *Williamson County, Tennessee Miscellaneous Records*, Volume 3. Affidavit of Jonathan Magness.

51. Reid trial notes, 23.

52. *Ibid*.

53. *Ibid*, 15.

the presence of a man named Joseph Alexander "since the pending of this cause" and "that poor as he was he would give five hundred dollars to have old Magness hung."[54]

Harman Newsom, one of the sons of "old" Lewis Newsom, gave similar testimony. He stated that he saw his father and Jonathan Magness in the yard for half an hour before the gunshot and heard Jonathan say, "[L]et's go home, but take a drink first."[55] Harman heard Anderson say he "intended to kill every damn hog thief, cow thief, and land warrant counterfeit rat in the house" and that "by his maker he would kill them as they entered" the house of old Newsom.[56] When he heard Anderson threaten the Magnesses, Lewis Newsom told his son, "[L]ord have mercy on us, murder will be done." Harman asked, "who?" The father answered, "I can't tell you now," and reaching out he urged Perrygreen Magness to come out and "he would tell him of danger."[57] Harman Newsom also noted the presence of Alexander and claimed he had heard Alexander say that "rather than have five hundred dollars he would have it that old Magness was hung."[58]

Isaac (Ike) Williams testified that Anderson asked to go with him to Newsom's house, proposing to make friends with him and "buying negroes of me." He thought Anderson to be "a man of overbearing character" who "carried a dirk, and commonly put it to use." Upon cross-examination, Williams admitted that he had threatened Anderson's life and had drawn a pistol in a fray "with Casey Monday night." He also confessed that he had been tried for murder but was found guilty of the lesser charge of manslaughter.[59]

The defense called several of the Magness's neighbors as character witnesses. These were of the group that William Preston Anderson would mock in a November 17, 1810, letter to Andrew Jackson:

---

54. Lynch, comp., *Williamson County, Tennessee Miscellaneous Records*, Volume 3. Affidavit of Jonathan Magness.
55. Reid trial notes, 15.
56. Ibid.
57. Ibid, 16.
58. Lynch, 51.
59. Reid trial notes, 13.

>...if the trumpet of hell had been sounded, and a general Jubalee pervated the whole infurnal regions, such a lot of murderers, thieves and scoundrels, could not have appeared, as the Magnesses have to sware for them.[60]

A man named Hicks who was a neighbor to Jonathan Magness said that he "lived in a neighborly way with him" and David Magness was "a mighty good boy." Cader Dement testified to his honesty and William Lannum and Joseph Lannum both described him as a "good boy." Ransom Gwinn described David as "peaceable and industrious." Joseph Broadway, who lived seven miles from Jonathan Magness, testified that he heard Anderson say he would "kill all the Magnesses if he did not get his horses." Although Broadway said he hadn't lived by the Magnesses for long and didn't know much, he still declared that he believed David to be "a good boy."[61]

The prosecution called witnesses to counter these character witnesses. Richard Britton stated that he had known David for three years and that he had a "bad character generally." A Major Bradley who lived within six miles from David believed that people "had not very good opinion of him" and there was "general suspicion in the neighborhood that when a bad man, a counterfeiter, came in, old Magness took him to his house." John M. Peak testified that the Magnesses were "spoken of generally as bad people" and had known David "to have 2 or 3 scrapes." Alex McCulloch stated that he had heard the Magnesses "spoken of generally as rascals" and their house as "the harbor of rogues."[62]

The prosecution also called several witnesses to attest to the good character of Patton Anderson. Major Nally, Col. Ward, G. Williams, Esq., Ch. B. Neilson and Joseph Coleman, Esq. were all listed as character witnesses for him.[63] The most famous character witness—and the pivotal witness of the trial—was General Andrew Jackson.

---

60. Harold D. Moser, Sharon MacPherson, Charles F. Bryan Jr., editors. *The Papers of Andrew Jackson, Volume 2, 1804–1813.* Knoxville: University of Tennessee Press, 1985, 255.

61. Reid trial notes, 22.

62. *Ibid.*

63. *Ibid*, 20.

According the trial notes of John Reid, Jackson was called as a witness for the state.[64] There is no doubt that on direct examination, the popular man told of the virtues of his friend. But it is the cross examination by Felix Grundy that is remembered in history. When asked by Grundy to opine upon the character of Patton Anderson, who was known by all in attendance as a man with a terrible temper and an addiction to drunkenness, Jackson exclaimed, "Sir, my friend Patton Anderson was the natural enemy of villains and scoundrels!"[65] While his comment may well have cast the Magnesses as incorrigible reprobates, in the context of the trial, Jackson's testimony was actually damaging to the prosecution. Rather than describing his dear friend as someone who could have been counted upon to turn a cheek or hold his passions in check, he was admitting that the community understood Anderson was a man who would take the fight to his enemies. For the defense, the argument that David Magness could have reasonably believed that Anderson would kill his father, and needed defense, became stronger.

William Chambers wrote about Jackson's testimony that "Grundy made much of this in his summation to the jury." However, it seems just as likely that Grundy would have made his points against Jackson as many times as possible, including during the cross-examination phase of the trial. The notes of Grundy's closing arguments make no mention of this exchange. Whenever he chose to use Jackson's own words against the prosecution's case, it annoyed Jackson greatly. At one point in the trial, upon hearing his testimony used against the prosecution, Jackson pulled young Thomas Hart Benton to one side to complain that Grundy's exploitation were "not fair play." Jackson urged Benton to "skin Grundy alive on that point" as part of the summation for the prosecution. Benton purportedly replied, "I am afraid, General, that he has got us down, on that point—flat on our backs. I reckon we had better let it alone."[66]

After several days of witness testimony, both sides presented viewpoints to support their case. Now it was up to the great law-

---

64. Ibid.

65. Ibid. See also Parton, *Life of Andrew Jackson*, 344.

66. William Nisbet Chambers, *Old Bullion Benton: Senator from the New West*. Boston: Little Brown and Company, 1956, 36.

yers to convince the jury that theirs were the most reliable of the witnesses. The show part of the show trial was about to begin.

5

The Great Lawyers Battle for the Jury

After the testimony of the witnesses, the record of the trial turns to the arguments made to the jury. It is unclear which of the prosecution attorneys initially laid out the case for the jury. Some of the references in the record point to John Overton making the opening case. Jenkin Whiteside clearly made the closing presentation. It appears from the record that the John Haywood presented the initial defense positions and that Felix Grundy closed the defense with final arguments.

Typically in a criminal trial the prosecution will make a summary of their case against the defendant. The defense will then make closing arguments as to why there is not substantial evidence for the defendant's conviction and present alternative scenarios for the jury. The prosecution then gets the last word, and can rebut the arguments the defense makes in their closing arguments. John Reid's notes of the Magness trial are contained on loose pages and are, at points, incomplete, duplicative, and out of order. The author, to the best of his ability, has placed the arguments in the order they would have been presented at trial.

The Prosecution Makes Its Case

The prosecution first asked the jury to focus on ten things that they believed pointed to the guilt of David Magness:

1. He had borrowed pistols secretly,
2. He went to Bedford County "without necessity" when he was certain of meeting Anderson there,
3. He remained in Bedford County for 3 days without ostensible business,
4. He sat in secret conclave on the log,
5. He put away his pistols on Tuesday, and carried them concealed on his arm on Wednesday,
6. He carried his pistols with his brother Perrygreen as he entered Newsom's house,
7. He sat, silent, collected, dark on the bench, with pistols,
8. The slyness with which he slipped up and fired,
9. His sudden flight and his prepared state of his arms,
10. His answers to those who questioned him after his apprehension. He said he had "no wife and children to weep for this little act." and "if no insult now—has been heretofore." He said to Philips, "you know all about it," to Bradford, "was willing to follow Anderson but not to meet him," and to Drake, "somebody in the room more to blame than I am."[1]

The prosecution also argued that David Magness had reasons for wanting Anderson dead. The prosecutors reminded the jury of the "general hostility of Anderson to all villains, of whom his

---

1. Reid, 24.

father's family was a notable part; and his father's house the place of rendezvous" and "the prosecution of the land warrant counterfeiters; the development of which threatened to involve prisoner and all his family."

The prosecution argued that David Magness couldn't claim self-defense after being threatened by Anderson because "Anderson was not even looking at him" when he fired. They asserted that Magness was not defending his father's life because "his father was in no danger."[2]

The prosecution also attacked the testimony of Jordan Reeves, the brother-in-law of the defendant, and the key witness for the defense. They mocked Reeves's claim as a religious man and suggested that he perjured himself.[3] In what appeared to be a description of Reeves, the prosecution stated:

> Watching the dead body of Anderson; in hopes no doubt that some half uttered sound may escape his lifeless lips that preying can distort into the justification of his murderers. Can the deep caverns of hell vomit forth a monster more foul than this? A demon more irascible than him who professing the religion of Christ, is yet the helpmate of thieves?—the associate of murderers—and with the prisoner seeks the vale of death unto an innocent man and who, after all, deliberately walked into the sanctuary of Justice, and there in the presence of God and his country, deliberately heaped praying on the top of perjury until, until, his own brethren have to cry out against him?"[4]

The prosecution laid out several specific instances where Reeves had been wrong from their perspective.[5] He was wrong in saying that Casey took hold of Anderson from behind and drew him back one step. He was wrong that Anderson had his dirk raised, was

2. *Ibid*, 25.
3. *Ibid*, 26.
4. *Ibid*, 26, 27.
5. *Ibid*, 28.

struggling to get forward, was swearing he would kill old Magness, and was at a distance less than four feet. Finally, the prosecution argued that Reeves was wrong when saying that old Magness kept his position, and went out at the south door.

The prosecution lawyer noted "the advocate who opened the defense, Mr. Haywood, would tell us that Reeves was supported by indifferent witnesses in all his statements."[6] However, he questioned, "who corroborates him in the circumstances of Anderson putting the stick in David's hand? Who in saying 'I'll kill David' to a stranger? Who?!"[7]

The prosecution railed, "Jordan [Reeves] is still unsupported except by vehement protestations, specious declamation, and loud but empty appeals to his former good standing in society." Presumably it was Whiteside who impeached Jordan Reeves with a ferocious attack:

> [Reeves] made out too good a case for the prisoner to have it—his testimony—thrown up without an effort to preserve it; and the renowned advocate who is to follow me will certainly undertake the defense of that man's testamentary credit—all wretched, disparate and miserable as it is. To him then do I address myself. I ask him to tell me who has supported Reeves in the story of Eskridge trembling in the court house? Who in that pitiful lie about taking the stick out of Dave's hand? Who in the threat made to the stranger man that he wanted to kill David? And who supports him in his tale of the last act, when Anderson was presented as standing on the seam of the floor, his arm uplifted to strike, making violent efforts to break forward over Casey; the old Man within 3 feet some odd inches of him; and a dreadful threat piercing from his mouth at the moment the pistol fires? Who supports Jordan in these circumstances wherever he has been so decisively without virtue not only by the states witnesses, but likewise by the most respectable of those who have been called by the defendant himself?

6. *Ibid*, 31.
7. *Ibid*, 29.

But witnesses have been called to tell us the character of Jordan; and can any man forget the remark of Mr. McCormick? That remark which of itself has ruined the credit of Jordan, and sent him naked and un-acquitted from the presence of this jury.

But I wanted no witness to tell me the character of Jordan. He has drawn a full length portrait of himself in the evidence which he has delivered to you. He is a religious man, a man of the house of God, and yet he gets his wife from that house which is no other than a den of thieves. Then he travels from Wilson County to Nashville to bail that villain Eskridge out of jail. Arrived at Bedford County whither he came without necessity, what does he do there? He fixes himself on the trail of Anderson; dogs him into all parts of the town; catches up his every word and gesture; repeats them to David Magness: and then lays them up in his faithful memory to be retold here to you. And when the last act of the tragedy is about to be performed, does he not himself tell you that he took his stand in the midst of the assassins; and never quitted his part 'til the victim was sacrificed and laid upon the altar. Even when his brother-in-law had fled, when the house was deserted, when the enraged multitude in the yard were threatening death to his relations, still this faithful witness remains at his watch post."[8]

The prosecution continued:

The counsel, who promised to show the consistency of Reeve's testimony, have failed. I ask you if you have not marked in his statement that bias which was to be expected. What has he proved? That Anderson stood not more than 4 feet from Old Magness? Other witnesses, who saw Anderson after he had, declare it could not be so. Reaves has stated more—that in the instant Anderson received [the fatal shot], in that instant he was threatening the old man—It is clear his evidence was made out to support a made out case—He states further that the old

8. *Ibid*, 31–33.

man was in imminent danger when the prisoner shot—that Anderson had his hand up with [the] dirk in his hand [and] stood in so appalling an attitude that it was to be expected that [in an] instant the dirk would have been plunged to his heart. Do any other witnesses say same thing? They tell you he was at nearest 8 feet. I do not mean to say Reeves has ever been advised with on this subject, but it manifestly appears he has made his evidence to[o]![9]

In the trial notes of John Reed, there are rebuttal points made to certain parts of the testimony in record. It is difficult to know exactly who they are focused upon, but they are interesting nonetheless. In response to an instance in the record at "page 27, the prosecution asked:

> Was this the effect of accident? Was this combination the work of chance? Or rather is it not an evidence that those who had begun by plundering meant now to finish their work by covering themselves with blood. Unhappy and now! Was it not enough that villains should deprive you of your property, but must your life also be taken from you because your spirit would not submit to be plundered by them?"[10]

At "page 29," the prosecution asked:

> Can the counsel for the accused give us an answer to these enquiries, for the witnesses have totally failed to do so? Can they account in any rational manner for this conduct, so totally at war with the defense which they have set up for their client? [Unclear] gentlemen had been permitted to have offered counsel to those able advocates who have appeared for the prisoner [he] should have advised them to lay out a small part of their

---

9. *Ibid*, 39.
10. *Ibid*, 29.

strength in clearing up these suspicious facts, instead of exhausting themselves and splitting open thin threats, in vain.[11]

The prosecution argued at "page 40":

> But a topic of defense has been drawn from a serious source. The very enormity of the prisoner's guilt is made by one of his counsel, this excuse of his crime. It is said if he had wanted to murder Anderson he would have fell upon him in some secret place, and not then have killed him in open day, in the midst of a multitude, in the face of the court itself? Ah Gentlemen, blush for my country when I am forced to tell you that the time when guilt would hide its head is passed away. Villainy no longer seeks concealment. Crime has thrown off her mask. The genius of assassination stalks through the country and bathes itself in blood. On all sides of us we hear of pistols, dirks and thieves? Of homicides and murder! Yet where is the instance in which the sword of Justice hath fallen on the neck of the [guilty]?[12]

At one point, the prosecutor lamented:

> Trials in a court of Justice have become nothing but solemn mockeries to legitimate the crimes of the greatest offenders. A little perjury and a little sophistry is enough to raise a doubt in the minds of the Jury, and then the villain must be turned loose to continue his depredation on the human race. Villains attend the trials of each other. Impunity gives confidence. They learn to commit crimes according to law. And thus it is that the greatest crimes are committed among us without compunction in the perpetrator or abhorrence in the public.[13]

---

11. *Ibid.*
12. *Ibid*, 27.
13. *Ibid.*

The Defense Responds

There is a record in the notes of John Reid of two long and similar speeches made by members of the collective defense counsel. They had similar arguments, but the language of the first speech was more technical than the second and includes more points of law. The first speech focused on the expertise of John Haywood which was the precedential laws of the land, i.e. legal precedents. Further, Whiteside references Haywood as giving parts of the first speech in his closing arguments. The second speech is filled with flourish and the type of rhetoric for which Felix Grundy was known. Also, in the record the second speech appears to be followed by "Whiteside in continuation" and Whiteside makes many references to comments recently given by Grundy.

The first speech, very likely the words of John Haywood, is found in order in Reid's notes:

> I rise not gentlemen to entreat your compassion or to implore your mercy; and I had been well I think, if no attempt had been made by the Counsel for the prosecution to enlist your feelings or excite your prejudices. There is no man where goodness I esteem more highly than Mr. Overton's—but his conduct on this occasion has surely been improper. Why has he introduced the Bible? Was it to excite unfavorable prepossession by the prisoner? By mingling the feelings of parley in the investigation of his cause? And Gentlemen—if there be a religious man on that jury, and after such no doubt the Bible was introduced, I beg him to remember that he who errs on the side of mercy may hope to be forgiven.—Gentlemen; are not the laws of our own country sufficiently severe by those who in wickedness violate them?—Are not its denunciations sufficiently heavy against the Murderer of [illegible] subjects? Why then resort to The Bible? It is by the laws of our own country that the unfortunate accused must now stand or fall, and not by the precepts of that sacred book. And why too gentlemen; were the clothes of the deceased brought in? Has not the evidence been sufficiently pointed to establish guilt upon

him? And must the [illegible] of your compassion supply its deficiencies. Gentlemen, I call upon you to be cool—collected and deliberate—Remember that ere long you must stand before the sovereign judge of the world as the unhappy accused now stands before you—to be judged according to your deserts.

It is a solemn duty which you owe to yourselves dispassionately to enquire whether your minds [are] under the influence of any prepossessions versus the prisoner – whether the rumors calculated out of doors, or the insinuations which have been read in this house have left behind them any impression—If so, it is your duty to banish them all. Believe nothing but what has been declared to you in evidence; and believe not, I entreat you, that this man is connected with a set of thieves. Which evidence of it do you have but the suspicions of Overton? I revere the goodness of that man's heart—but his suspicions are surely not to be evidence for you.—Let us then proceed to an examination of the law and this suspect and apply it to this case as made out by these witnesses. The prisoner stands indicted of murder. Murder, gentlemen, is divisible into several species—Justifiable homicide which is not punishable at all — Manslaughter which is punished with burning. The last and highest is that of Murder. The punishment of which is death. Murder is the voluntary killing a person of malice prepense. Malice which is an essential ingredient in the offence imparts in the legal acceptation, imparts a wickedness which includes a circumstance attending an act that cuts off all excuse—If then the act of slaying Patton Anderson be proven to have been committed by the prisoner on a preconcertion without sufficient provocation, I agree it is murder.

[In] 4 Black 195 Murder is defined "when a person of sound memory and discretion unlawfully kills any reasonable creature in being and under the King's peace with malice afore-thought either express or implied. The same author in page 199 of the same book says that express malice is when with a sedate, deliberate mind and formed design doth kill another; which formed design is evidenced by external circumstance, discovering that inward intention; as lying in wait—antecedent menaces former grudges, and concerted schemes to do him some bodily harm. If therefore from a fair examination of the evidence you shall be led to believe that the death of Anderson originated in a formed design, or concerted scheme existed in the bosom of the prisoner, it is murder. But if you shall believe that such formed design or concerted scheme existed in the mind of the prisoner—If you shall believe, as I persuaded myself you will, that the death of Anderson arose from sufficient provocation offered by the deceased himself, then is his offense not murder—but manslaughter. 4 Black 191 [says] "So also if a man be greatly provoked as by pulling his nose or other great indignity and immediately kills the aggressor no this is not excusable or defended—yet neither is it murder." And gentlemen: it is everywhere laid down in the books that if two quarrel and one provokes the other so as to put him in a temporary fury and he kills, it is not murder. So great a regard does the law pay to the frailty of human nature. And gentlemen: This is not only the language of the law: it is equally the language of reason. You are then to inquire what it is that the law considers a sufficient provocation.

In 2d McNal 564 it is laid down that words of reproach are not sufficient to free the slayer from the offense of murder, unless they be accompanied with an assault—but if there be an assault it is only manslaughter. This principle was also recognized in the case of Morley [in] East 213. Mr. Overton in reading these authorities did not proceed far enough. He was cautious always to stop as soon as he had read that words could not constitute a sufficient provocation,—without going on to the end of the sentence where he would have found that the words could not yet that an assault might. And: gentlemen: This doctrine is not only laid down in the authorities which I have read—but it is clearly advanced in Hale's pleas of the Crown 456. And it is admitted on every hand, that a greater criminal lawyer never sat on the English bench. Hale lived when parties raged—and all parties adored him. He says it was agreed by all the judges that menace of bodily harm might convert the offence of killing into Manslaughter.

I have quested these authorities to show that when the slaying proceeds from an assault made, or a menace of great bodily harm, it can never be murder. And to these authorities many more might be added. In Foster 290 it is said that words of threatening with reason to believe they will be followed up by killing will reduce the offence of the slayer to manslaughter and again in Hale 453 it is laid down that words of reproach are not sufficient to free the killer from the offense of murder unless they be followed up by an assault—Thereby raising the clear implication that when so followed up the offense of killing cannot be murder.

Having shown you what is murder, and what is manslaughter, let us now inquire of justifiable homicide. Foster 273 states that in justifiable homicide the injured party may repel force by force in defense of his person habitation or property by one who manifestly intendeth and endevoureth by violence or surprise to commit a known felony upon either. In these cases he is not obliged to retreat, but may pursue his adversary till he findeth himself out of danger, and if a conflict between them be happeneth to kill, such killing is justifiable. Now gentlemen I contend if the prisoner at the bar has had good reason to apprehend danger to his father he is as much to be excused for having interfered to save him as though that danger had been real. In McNal 562 the same doctrine is adopted. And in the King vs Cooper it was ruled by the Court that if one assail a house with a view of committing burglary, or to kill any therein, a party within the hours (although he be not the master, but a lodger a sojourner therein) kill him who made the assault, it is not felony, but excusable (Cro: Car: 544 · | East 15· Car:) And if a lodger may interpose in a case like this, may not the son in a much stronger case—in attempt to kill his father interpose for a much stronger reason? In Mawgridge's case it was said by the great Hale that it was justifiable and lawful in Cope to return the bottle; for he that hath manifested he hath malice to another is not fit to be trusted with a dangerous weapon in his hand. In the case before you Anderson had drawn his dirk—Mawgridge had drawn his sword in the case I have cited—Mawgridge had manifested symptoms of malice and enmity—So had Anderson; and the one no more than the other, should have been trusted with the dangerous weapon in his hand. Such is the decision of that able judge; and such I doubt not will be yours.—It has been decided also that persons rudely forcing themselves into a room in a tavern as this will if this company in possession—one of the assailants is killed in the scuffle—this is justifiable homicide. And such the case which you are now considering is a thousand times stronger in behalf of the prisoner—I have read those authorities to show you what is justifiable homicide.

Apply them to the present case; and you will readily perceive that if the life old Magness was in danger from the deceased that the son in killing of nothing more than excusable homicide and of the danger to the father was not indeed real. Still if you believe the son had good reason to apprehend that danger to be great, he is as much to be excused as though that danger had been real. The correctness of this doctrine I conceive to be unquestionable; and to illustrate it I will assume a case. Father and son are in town together – father receives a sum of money—son tells him to be on his guard as he returns, by robbers. Son in a [frolic] pushes on ahead and waylays the road—on the coming up of the father, springs out – demands his money in an altered voice and presents an empty pistol at his breast—[the] father kills [him]—this is justifiable homicide; and yet, the danger here was not real—but only imaginary. In the trial of Selfridge it was decided that when it is justly to be apprehended from the nature of the attack, that it is designed to take away life, the killer is justifiable though it should afterwards appear that no felony was intended. (Self ·160· —)

This then is the principle which I wish to fix in your mind and which I wish you carry with you when you retire to your chambers. That a man is as much to be excused who kills to prevent a felony which he believes, on good grounds is about to be committed, as if that felony were really designed—and that if the son in the present case may well be presumed to have thought his father's life in danger he stands on the same ground for his justification, as though what he imagined had really been true. For in all the books which trial of the relations between father and son it is expressly said a son that therefore may kill in defense of his father and that in fighting to save him, he stands on the same ground that the father would if he fought for himself. (Hale 484 · 4 · Black 186 | Hale 142 ·F274)

Let us come now to the evidence and apply it to the law of this case. And first I will say a word or two concerning the confessions of the prisoner, which have been professed in with so much earnestness against him. All the law books which speak of the confessions of a prisoner say—that but very little regard should be paid to them by the Jury: On the present occasion I say that no regard whatever should be paid to them. Just reflect on the situation of the prisoner at the time he made those declarations which have been relied on, and I am sure you will believe with me that they are entitled to no weight. They were made after he committed the act—after he was arrested—when he was confined in chains—when he was surrounded by his enemies—when he must have been agitated and alarmed in the high degree—and when he was liable for all these reasons to misapprehend the questions which were put to him. Are the declarations of a man in circumstances like these to operate against his life? Is it to be expected that they will convey the clear and naked truth when all was turmoil and uproar within occasioned by the act of dread and unforeseen necessity which he had been compelled to perform—and heightened by the fear of immediate danger which he might well have apprehended from some irritated friend of the deceased—is it to be wondered at that he should have spoken incoherently and at random. Must not that man be driven to desperation and madness who before his enemies will make confessions that shall take away his life? And if he should make them, gentlemen, you are not to regard them; such is the human language of our law—and such is the language of that sacred book which has been introduced for another purpose. Horten in page 243 says that hasty confessions made to persons having no authority to examine are the weakest and most suspicious of all evidence. Proof may be too easily procured—words are often misreported.

Whether through ignorance—inattention or malice it mattereth not to the Defendant; he is equally affected in either case. And they are extremely liable to misconstruction. And withal this evidence is not in the ordinary course of things to be disproved by that sort of negative evidence by which the proof of plain facts may be and often is confronted"—the same principle has uniformly governed the decisions in North Carolina—And in Fisher's case when a burglary has been committed and watches stolen, but no evidence to fix the stealing upon the defendant but by his own confession freely and voluntarily made to the Magistrate who examined him; it was declared by the court to be an established rule of law that the mere confession of a crime without other evidence to report it is not sufficient to convict a prisoner unless—he should again confess the fact by pleading guilty to the indictment—Then authorities will show what little regard ought to be paid by you to those confessions of the prisoner which have been relied on as the true? Indications of his guilt; And the evidence which has been introduced respecting confession is I think peculiarly fitted to convince you of the propriety of the decisions of the law. Just advert [paper edge clipped] to it for a moment. Drakes says that after the prisoner was arrested he refused to shake hands with him, the prisoner observed that there was some person in that house more to be believed than himself. Drake fancied his allusion was to the old man—his father, but I ask if there is not greater reason to think the allusion was to Drake himself—who was it that commenced the conversation with the old man, about [the] trial, Riggs, and the counterfeit land warrant? Who was it that brought up (inadvertently and without design) the quarrel with the deceased and old Mangess?—It was Drake—Drake was innocent and yet he had been the unhappy and unknowing instrument."[14]

---

14. *Ibid*, 48–57.

THE GREAT LAWYERS BATTLE FOR THE JURY

The second long speech by the defense attorneys appears in the notes of John Reid out of order, but the language appears to be that of Felix Grundy. Grundy used passionate rhetoric such as when he described Anderson as "the most violent and turbulent man that could disgrace this country" and David Magness' shooting of Anderson as understandable "for the same reason you might arise against a Mohawk who had threatened your life."[15] While the substance of the second speech is similar to that of the first, it is the style of Grundy that is seen:

> I rise not, gentlemen, to implore your mercy or enlist your passion. It is your judgments and not your sympathies which I would address on this occasion.—If the prisoner be indeed guilty of murder—If the deceased has really fallen victim to a scheme preconceived, by the prisoner to take away his life, he stands exposed to the heaviest animadversions of the law and we do not solicit his acquittal. But if the act for which he is now arraigned was not of his own seeking—but forced upon him by the deceased himself—if he was prompted to commit it by an instinctive impulse to save a father from a danger which threatened his life—If gentlemen he obeyed only the suggestion of that innate principle which Nature for the wisest purposes has implanted in the bosom of every child, then I trust you will not doom his person to destruction nor his name to infamy.
>
> Your situation, gentleman, is a serious one indeed. It is cloaked with the most awful responsibility. The issues of life and death are in your hands. I am well aware of the rumors which have gone abroad in the world concerning the unfortunate transaction which has brought the prisoner to your bar—and I do know how well those rumors were calculated to excite against him the most unfavorable prejudices. Gentlemen, I do conjure you to banish every prepossession. By every motive which can influence the integrity of men I call upon you to forget all that you may have heard out of doors—to enter

---

15. *Ibid*, 160.

upon the examination of this solemn question, with minds diverted of every prejudice—to examine the testimony coolly and deliberately, that by comparing it with the law, you may be enabled to pronounce such a decision as your consciences shall always approve.

Homicide gentlemen is of three kinds—justifiable, excusable and felonious—The first has no share of guilt at all, the second very little; but the third is the highest crime against the law of nature that man is capable of committing (4 Blak 178). This last is the offence with which the prisoner stands charged. He is charged with the murder of Patton Anderson. Murder, gentlemen, is the killing [of] a reasonable creature with malice prepense (Hawk 49) which means an intention deliberately formed to take away life. Manslaughter is the unlawful killing another without malice. It is your duty then to ascertain from the evidence under what species of homicide the act committed by the prisoner is to be classed. And permit me to ask in the outset, if you have perceived in that evidence anything which can bring it within the definition of murder? Have you perceived in it any of those symptoms of settled malice and cool determination by which the law distinguishes this worst of offences from all others? No such feature have I been able to discover.

The history of the transaction divested of all those extraneous circumstances, which the ingenuity of the counsel for the prosecution have thrown around it, is shortly this. The prisoner, his father and brother, on their way to the Muscle Shoals had occasion to call at Shelbyville where the circuit court was in session, on business. Anderson was also there. On Wednesday, Anderson with Drake and the prosecutor went into the house of Newsom for the purpose of taking a drink of grog. Jonathan Magness (the father) about the same time had entered the house for the same purpose: but perceiving Anderson, and knowing that his heart had long been full of bitterness toward him, he retires to the distant part of the room that he might be entirely out of his way; and there enters into a peaceable conversation with Drake. But his circumspection did not await him.

Anderson follows him up in order to insult him—which he presently does in the most offensive manner. The old man, who though disposed to peace, was no coward, repels the insult, in terms as warm, though not so bitter, as those in which it had been offered. The prisoner who just then was making ready to set out on his journey, hears the noise, and enters the room with his saddle bags and holsters on his arm. Quietly he takes a seat on the opposite side, in hopes that the quarrel might blow over without any dangerous consequences. But his hopes were doomed to disappointment. The quarrel, warm at first, instantly becomes violent. Anderson in a paroxysm of rage draws a dirk from his side—swears he will kill!—and raises the hand which grasped it, to execute the threat. Here was a crisis the most eventful for the son that the human mind can conceive. How was he to have acted? How should a son not destitute of every feeling of filial affection have acted in that awful moment? There stood an aged father ready to be sacrificed in an instant, to the infuriated passions of a man who had long sworn his destruction. Was the son to stand calmly by and witnessed the sacrifice? Was that a moment for wavering and hesitation? No gentlemen, when in that perilous moment the prisoner interposed to save the life of a father, he acted as every son, placed in his situation would have acted. And yet he is called a murderer. Whether he be so or not you are to be his Earthly Judges. There is another Judge to whom he must one day appeal, and whose sentence will be unnerving. In this world he must abide your decision. Your verdict must establish whether he shall be classed with the worst of malefactors in whose envenomed malice of heart, [illegible] death of an unoffending fellow being is conceived, long before it is executed—whether he merits the same punishment with them—whether his name like theirs shall go down to posterity disgracing all who bear [hear] it!

Was his motive like theirs? Are the sentiments which animate the bosom of a son when he interposes to save an aged father from danger and from death, to be classed with the feelings which urge the highwayman to his midnight assault upon the unsuspecting traveler? Are they to be classed with those which preside in the mind of the prisoner when he sits collected and dark over his crucible mingling the potion which tomorrow shall freeze up the avenues of his neighbor's heart? Surely not. Surely there is an everlasting difference between the characters—a difference recognized both by reason and the Law—a difference that shows the same view can with no propriety be applied to both. In the act of the prisoner where is the envisioned malice—the cold blooded deliberation so essential to the constitution of murder. It was Nature herself that put the pistol in his hand: To save the life of a father when assailed by danger, the laws of Heaven and man excuse. But this is cold language they commend; they enforce it as a duty. Was the prisoner influenced by any other motive?—did he aim at any other object?—We are told (not by the witnesses but by the prosecution counsel) that his motives and his object were different—that he had premeditated the death of the deceased. And that he went to Shelbyville for the purpose of executing the scheme he had digested. Dreadful indeed is the charge—but gentlemen by what evidence is it supported? By the evidence of Tune? Give to the evidence of Tune the most unlimited credit, and it is altogether insufficient to support the charges. What was that evidence? About an hour before the catastrophe he saw the prisoner and his brother (Perry G.) going into the house of Newsom. Perry G. asked the prisoner if his pistols were in order, who answered in the affirmative. Perry G then observing one of them to be placed wrong in the holster went forward and righted it. This was the evidence of Tune as he gave it on the application to counsel and as he has given it here. Gentlemen, is not this feeble evidence to support the charge of preconcerted Murder! A pistol is placed wrong in the holster and no man shall meddle with it lest forsooth he should subject both himself and his friend to the charge of premeditated guilt!!

But ridicule, though proverbially the test of truth, is not the means by which we shall seek the acquittal of the prisoner. I say that the evidence of Tune, though it were to receive the most unbounded confidence is altogether insufficient to substantiate the charge which has been made. It could not even serve as a link to supply a charm in a chain of evidence. But gentlemen this evidence poor as it is, is entitled to no credit whatever. It was told by a man unworthy of belief—it was told in a manner to deprive it of credit—it was contradicted by other witnesses and was contradicted by this witness himself. No longer than the day after he had given this evidence, he expressed his sorrow for what he had done—declared he had sworn too hard, and that if it were to do again he should act differently. Yet sorry as the unfortunate Mr. Tune was,—this arch key of the prosecution—he found it necessary (for he had heard of the punishment of perjury) to preserve consistency of statement and again to depose to the same facts. Gentlemen, is this man to be believed?—a man who voluntarily contradicts the statements he had made on oath?—But passing by this for a moment I ask if you could require stronger counteracting testimony to his evidence than the manner in which he gave it in. Whoever saw such hesitation, such faltering, such stammering? Whoever saw such a countenance of conscious guilt in a witness? I am sure the counsel for the prosecution were themselves ashamed of having introduced him. Did you gentlemen, I ask again, in all your attendance upon courts ever before observe in a witness a manner so embarrassed?—a countenance so strongly indicative of that inward uneasiness which a man may be expected to feel who designs by his evidence to support a made out case, but is at the same time fearful of being caught in an inconsistency and yet this is the evidence which is to support the charge of preconcerted murder? By the evidence of this man it was triumphantly foretold the scheme of murder was to be developed and the prisoner condemned.

Let us enquire then by what other evidence this preconceived scheme to take away the life of the deceased can be established upon the prisoner. Why it has been asked if no such design was meditated by him did, he carry his pistols about him? Is not this circumstance sufficiently accounted for? Have you not been told that he was about setting out on his journey to the Shoals—and that he had gotten his holster and saddle bags for this purpose?—Again it has been said that at the time he fired upon the deceased his father was in no danger—that Anderson was too far removed from him, and was besides in the hands of Casey. Tell me gentlemen, when a man like Anderson as remarkable for desperate rashness as he was for personal prowess had drawn a dirk from his side, and sworn in his wrath that he would plunge it in the bosom of the old man—tell me, you who knew him, if there was no danger—Tell me if there was none to be apprehended? When did the deceased ever make a threat which he was too timid to execute? Within what bounds was his resentment ever curbed? Did he not hold the whole country in awe? Was he not the most impetuous? The most violet, the most dangerous private citizen that ever lived in any country governed by law? Long had the most deadly animosity influenced his bosom against the Magnesses—Often had he threatened their lives. And now a crisis had arrived when all the infuriated passions of his bosom were collected to [*illegible under ink blot*]. And yet we are told that old Magness was not in danger? Ah: gentlemen in the hour of tranquility, when danger is far from us, it loses all its terrors.

We can speculate conversely with this calmness of philosophers, but well convinced am I that if on that day one of those gentlemen had stood in the place of Magness willingly would he have resigned all the honors and the emoluments he now has. But we are told that he was in the hands of Casey.—And have not those gentlemen themselves told you and told you truly, that he could in an instant have broken from his hold and committed the outrage he threatened if he had been so disposed? Yes indeed! Casey was poor security with all his operations for the safety of the old man. Was the son to wish the life of a father on such grounds? Was he to wait until some others should invite their efforts with Casey's to hand off the blow? Was this a time for him to calculate on the possible ways by which his father might escape? Was he to wait for the concurrence of fortunate circumstances to affect it? Was this a moment, I ask when a son should have paused and deliberated?! Little does he know of the strength of filial attachment who believes it. *[Illegible word]* in his bosom must be the best feelings of our nature. Execrated through life would the prisoner deservedly have been had his father perished, while he paused to deliberate.

But for the justification of the prisoner, it is of no importance whether the danger to the father were real or imaginary. Could he have doubt concerning to reality? Did not the prosecutor himself believe it to be real? Why also did he interpose? Did not Montgomery and did not Newsom leave there that they might not be witnesses to a spectacle of murder? And the son was to be more skeptical than any of these? Was he to wait with folded arms and a heart at ease until the danger became more threatening before he interfered!! Gentlemen of what materials would they have had this son to be composed! He was to be motionless and unaffected when the life of his father was assailed. In that moment they would have him to be a frigid calculator of the degrees of danger and of the possible ways in which an escape might be affected? Let us suppose him then to be as cold as they would have him. Let us suppose him with all the deliberation of a layman laying down his promises and deducing his conclusions, before he proceeded to act. Would not his conduct still have been the same? Was there any apparent means to save the life of his father but try the most energetic interposition? Was not the dagger drawn? Was it not lifted? Would it not in an instant have done its work of destruction? Was that a time for halfway measures? Was it a time for lukewarm interposition? No gentlemen, moderate or tardy exertions could have been of no avail. Before it worked its effect, the mischief it intended to prevail had been already accomplished. Whether then the prisoner acted in obedience to that instinctive feeling which nature for the wisest purposes has implanted in the bosom of every child—or whether he pursued the more cool conclusions of reasons, his conduct is equally to be justified. Neither the evidence of Casey nor the conduct of the prisoner himself immediately precedent to the catastrophe can warrant son in saying that he dad preconceived the death of the deceased. But a resort has been had to the evidence of Griffin for the purpose of establishing that fact. The witness had borrowed the pistols from him, for the purpose of it has been said of executing the act, for which he now stands arraigned—But gentlemen how uneventably—how ungenerously has it been said. Is the carrying of pistols conclusive proof of a design to commit murder? But gentlemen, is not the carrying of them sufficiently accounted for on this occasion by the evidence? By the evidence of Griffin himself? Was not the prisoner going on a journey to the shoals with a drove of horses? And is it unusual, or is it improper for men on a journey of this kind to go armed? Did he not tell Griffin this, at the time he borrowed the pistols? Did he not borrow them expressly for this journey? And Griffin, who was intimate with the prisoner, was with him for several days, at the house of his father previous to his setting out on this journey. Did he ever utter a threat against the deceased?—Did he express any resentment towards him?—Did he ever mention his name? No gentlemen he uttered no threat—he expressed no resentment. How forced and unnatural is it then from the bare borrowing of the pistols for an expressed occasion to infer that they were designed for the destruction of the deceased? How ground up and uncharitable is the insinuation. But why did he call at Bedford Courthouse which was somewhat out of his direct course? Did he not tell Griffin previously that business would compel him to call there on his way? And is it unusual for men on a journey to turn a little aside from their main course to accomplish a necessary business and thereby save the trouble of a second trip?! Cheerless gentlemen must be the prospect of the prosecution when they are compelled to resort to circumstances like these to procure the conviction of a man whom they hate; and sanguinary indeed must that government be, where circumstances are received as proof of preconceived guilt. No gentlemen the prisoner meditated no wrong. He uttered no threats. No desire of revenge rankled in his bosom. But far different towards him and his father were the feelings and the conduct of the deceased. Often had he threatened their lives. Often tried he called Heaven to witness his determination to pursue them to destruction. Had not the prisoner heard of these threats? And was it not excusable—was it not wise and proper—that he should go armed in his defense. Away then with this tale of the pistols; it only proves the desperate ground on which the prosecution rests. I have said that the deceased was bent upon the destruction of the prisoner and his father. And, gentlemen, there is no principle better known in the law than that where a man arrives at the commission of an unlawful act every consequence is chargeable upon himself. It was the deceased himself who brought about the catastrophe in which he perished. Taking the life of Jonathan Magness he was himself slain. Was an occasion sought either by the prisoner or his father to bring on the dispute which eventuated so fatally? Did they not strive to slow it?! Had not the old man taken a seat in a remote part of the room?! Had he uttered a word to the deceased when he was attacked by the deceased? Did he not request him to retire? Does any part of the conduct of father show a wish to bring on an encounter?! Was it not forced upon them?! They who strove for peace, or the man who proclaimed war! Gentlemen, it is not my wish to stigmatize the memory of the deceased. I lament the fate to which his own imprudence urged him. We have been told he was a warm friend, and I shall not deny it. But was he not a most bitter enemy, was not his temper too revengeful – his hatred too inveterate? Did not passion the most violent and tempestuous triumph too much in his mind? But I will tread lightly on his ashes. All I wish to show is that the extremity in which he perished was of his own procurement. I wish to show that the unhappy accused, strong as the current of popular opinion may bear against him, is no murderer. His conscience I am sure must acquit him of the charge, and the laws of our country re-echo the assurance.

This is a day of awful anxiety and solicitude to the defendant—A day which can never be forgotten by him, while the lamp of life is permitted to burn, and while reason holds his empire—yet I may, say of humble hope and confidence in the justness of his defense, and the integrity and impartiality of this jury, shield it with a consciousness of his own rectitude and the parity of his intentions my client can have no dread—for what has an honest man to fear? (and though dishonor may have been attributed to some of the conversions of my client, yet it cannot attach to him) and what may not an honest man hope for? Envy and malice may point their deadly shafts at his reputation—the thunder of calamity may burst over his head and its lightening flash under his feet—yet is he unhurt!

The consciousness, that he acted from necessity, not sought for, but imposed upon him by the conduct of the deceased from whom danger and enormous bodily harm were to be apprehended—That he acted in advancement of justice, to prevent the murder of his father—That he acted from the strong impulse of filial love, which to have controlled by a passive submission to the murderous view of the deceased, would have degraded him below the level of a man—That he acted in obedience to nature's sovereign command which not to have obeyed would be treason against his own life, buoys him beyond despondency, and even the apprehension of danger.

From the known benignity of the judge who presides upon this trial, whose charge, as the polar star, will guide your enquiries as to law of this case—From the impartiality of this jury, whose prejudices, if such they entertained, were left at the threshold of this sanctuary of justice—and whose minds cannot be influenced by the uncommon [*illegible word*] with which this prosecution is prepared—from the confidence which my client feels I having done no more than this duty which he owed himself, his father, his God required—though he regrets that the necessity should have existed which compelled the act—He cheerfully consigns his fate, his future prospects, his honor, his life to your decision—decide as your conscience tell you is right—decide as the laws of nature and man have before decided—decide according to the golden rule of doing as you would be done unto—and I venture to speak without fear of contradiction, that your decision will be an acquittal."[16]

The Prosecution Closes Its Case

Whiteside presented the final arguments for the prosecution:

> No man ever prepared himself with more deliberation and caution for the destruction of a fellow being. He had as an extravagant price, furnished himself with the best brace of pistols which the country could afford—prepared balls,—and obtained a gourd of the best powder. Now I ask if all these warlike arrangements were made to resist a danger which he apprehended. Did he believe that Anderson would assail him? Why then was he never heard when travelling thus accoutered, or when at Shelbyville to express his fears! Did he tell Griffin when he borrowed the pistols that he apprehended danger from Anderson?—Did he avow that as his motive for borrowing them?—Did he to any human being ever explain his reason for this warlike array—And why should he have apprehended danger from Anderson? The threats which Anderson has been said to have uttered against the Magnesses, were always conditional and referred to his being able to establish their connection with Eskridge. Nor does it appear that the prisoner even heard of those threats—And it is very probable he did not—As he failed to communicate them to his confidential friend Wm. Griffin. But whether he had heard of those threats or not, it is very clear that he did not act upon them. Neither he nor the old man ever insinuated that they entertained such fears.
>
> Take then the motives which these men had to destroy the deceased—view the arrangements which were made to affect this purpose; and connect them with the prisoners declarations to Phillips—Bedford and Drake after that purpose had been accomplished, and I [illegible] to offer there never was

---

16. Ibid, 58, 59–62, 63–66.

a plainer case of murder made out in a court of Justice. Mr. Grundy however told you are right that he knew how you would decide—that he knew you would acquit the prisoner. How he came by this knowledge I cannot conjecture. I do hope this jury's determination to acquit the prisoner was not known to Mr. Grundy before they were impaneled. I do hope they entered that box without any predetermination either to acquit or condemn. Whatever zeal may have appeared on the part of the prosecutor I am sure it is the wish of none of us to see the prisoner condemned unless he be really guilty—Nor could his punishment gratify us if the laws of our country did not require it. But I would ask to what a condition of wretchedness we should be reduced if those laws may be violated with impunity—if Juries shall disregard their commands and listen only to the suggestions of sympathy and compassion. However you may commiserate the melancholy fate to which a fellow being has reduced that must not divert you from a calm and dispassionate investigation of the evidence. If the result of that investigation shall be a conviction of the prisoner's guilt, though it tear your breasts with anguish you must still pronounce him guilty. And who can doubt that this man is a murderer? If all other evidence were wanting his own confessions subsequent to the homicide must establish his guilt beyond all question. Just revert for a moment to the evidence of Phillips—can anything show more conclusively the design and motive with which the act was committed. In deed that evidence, when connected with other circumstances amounts in my mind to demonstration. The declarations of a prisoner when they proceed not from constraint the law considers as the most conclusive evidence by him—Declarations when not extorted by fear or induced by hope are presumed to flow from the genuine conviction of guilt. In this case neither the enticements of hope nor the terror of menace were resorted to, to extract the prisoner's declarations. They were made voluntarily and without solicitation. Would he then I ask, if he had believed and felt that he had performed a meritorious action have told Bradford that he wished he had had a pistol and had shot him. Was his language and conduct on this occasion such as conscious innocence produces? Were they not the clearest manifestations of inward guilt? Mr. Grundy has told you that he cares not what the law is in this case—that there are certain great and immutable principles in the constitution of man on which alone he shall seek the acquittal of the prisoner. Where he received this high dispensing power I am as much at a loss to conjecture as I am to ascertain how he came by the knowledge of what your verdict would be. But it is very well for Mr. Grundy's client that he is able to follow his defense on some other basis than the laws of our Country. Mr. Grundy was aware that by those laws he must forever stand; condemned—and it was certainly ingenious to seek some other refuge.

But notwithstanding his noisy declamation I trust that he has not persuaded you that you have the right—even if you could have the inclination to dispense with the laws of your country—with all the magic of his eloquence I should presume that he can hardly have convinced you that when a man is charged with a violation of the laws—and that charge is clearly established upon him by evidence that you have the right nevertheless to pronounce him not guilty? If we show that this man slew the deceased with that sort of mind which in law will constitute him a murderer we shall still expect a verdict notwithstanding the very terrible manner in which your feelings must have been lacerated and torn by the eloquence of Mr. Grundy. Mr. Phillips tells you that the witness, after the commission of the homicide, and after he was arrested appeared quite undaunted—quite unmoved. Yes gentlemen, that ferocity which prompted him to the dreadful deed had not subsided—He had attained the object of his wish—He had affected the grand purpose of his long preparation—and now he was ready to meet any fate that might be reserved for him. He tells one of the witnesses that though Anderson had not insulted him on this occasion he had been insulted by him previously. This insult still rankled in his bosom, and cooperated with other considerations to bring on the fatal catastrophe. To say that he slew the dreaded to rescue his father is out of the question. If that had been his would he not have avowed it—was it not the most laudable one by which he could be governed—and yet during all this time, he does not even suggest that this consideration actuated him at all. So far from this he expresses a different motive—your Mr. Phillips says he lived in Jefferson—You know how this affair originated. Did not this confession flow without constraint? Was he threatened, or was he enticed? Neither the one nor the other. He takes a drink of spirits. He composes his mind. He had killed the man whose death he had long meditated. He knew he deserve death and was prepared to meet it. But a miserable perversion was that of Mr. Haywood to say that the prisoner's allusion when he told Drake there was some person in the room more to blame than himself was to Drake himself. It would be an unnecessary waste of time to expose its absurdity. When Drake entered the room in Stone's house in which the prisoner was confined he offered him his hand—Drake sternly refuses to receive it. He attempts then to apologize to Drake for his conduct. "You know not the motives by which I have been led to the commission of this deed—there is one in this room more to blame than myself." That his allusion was to his father [is not in] doubt. It was the wish of the prisoner to convince Drake under whose influence he'd been prompted to kill his friend.

Connect the assemblage on the log with the circumstances which went before with the whole of these declarations that followed after. And no man on Earth who is willing to believe the truth can [have] doubt concerning it. Even if Anderson had killed old Magness still the prisoner is a murderer. His declarations clearly show the previous malice which existed in the prisoner's heart and that malice will constitute him a murderer however fortunate the pretense may have been in which he brought it to play. This candid open avowal of the prisoner after he had completed the object of his wishes is the most unquestionable evidence of the prisoner's motive and of that description of mind with which he committed the act.

Lawyers may quibble and declaim—they may conspire of chimeras and hobgoblins to frighten your imaginations—they may paint in the most vivid colors the alarm, perturbation, and turmoil of feeling which the prisoner must have experienced after committing the act—but these declarations flowing as they did without constraint or solicitations, must in spite of all their efforts remain an unerring evidence of the mala mens with which the prisoner assailed the life of the deceased—they are unmovable testimonials of his guilt. Having learnt what the law is in this case and having examined and weighed the evidence if you can still say that the prisoner is innocent, I can only observe that it is time for every good man to send to the state and have it in the possession of such men as the prisoner—his council and his jury. You have been told much of the necessity the son was under to kill the deceased in order to save his father; and I repeat that if the fact were so, it cannot operate to excuse the son of a design to take away the life of the deceased forever—only existed in his mind. No matter in what circumstances the act was committed, or what pretext existed to give a plausible coloring to it. The malice of the prisoner's mind must still constitute him a murderer; and this malice we have clearly shown to have existed both from the circumstances which went before and from those which followed the catastrophe. Recollect gentlemen the case of Oneby which has been read to you at length. In his case the declarations which established his guilt were made before he had slain Gower; and are not for that reason entitled to half the credit of declarations made subsequently to the killing. The mind of a man immediately before he commits an act of this kind may well be supposed to be greatly agitated; and unguarded expressions might naturally enough escape him. But after confessions made when the object of revenge has been attained—made like then of the prisoner at the bar when his heart was gratified and at care—when he had consummated the act of all his ambition in this world and was ready then to offer up his life as the atonement—there declarations can lead us into no mistake—They ascertain description of the offence with a certainty and perception that cannot be expected from any other kind of evidence. It is one of the rules of law that where two fight on equal terms, no matter who commences the assault, the offence of killing shall only be considered manslaughter. But only [*illegible*] fought on equal; and yet only after the most able trial that ever a man had was found guilty of murder. And why? Because the declarations which he had previously made established the malice of his mind and this malice constituted him a murderer. But I ask if that malice was so clearly shown in the case of Oneby as it has been in this of Magness. Have we not shown the existence of that malice a thousand times more strongly in the bosom of the prisoner? Just for a moment run a parallel between the cases. In the case of Oneby after the quarrel had commenced—After violence had been used after bottles had been thrown in an angry manner—after swords had been seized up and when the blood of Oneby might still be boiling with passion he tells Gower, damn you, I'll leave your blood. This declaration it was which was considered by the court as evidence of Oneby's malice and which made him a murderer. But was this declaration by any means so certainly indicative of malice as those which the prisoner at the bar made after he had slain the deceased and when anger and resentment could no longer have [lain] possessed a dwelling in his bosom. The declarations of the prisoner appear to have been made when he was unagitated by any violent passion, and influences by any extraordinary emotion—They made at a time when he was even amusing himself with the odd curiosity of the spectators—when he could laugh and smoke and drink. Thus calm and composed we hear him declaring to Mr. Phillip "You know [what] gave rise to this transaction—You who live in Jefferson know that though the prisoner did not insult me today he did on a former occasion." Here the gratification of an old grudge is the avowed motive of his conduct. Here is an unsought and voluntary admission of the malice by which he had been actuated. No obligation that he considered his father's life in danger and that he interfered to save it. This was an after-thought, it did not occur to him while truth was predominant in his mind and perhaps would never have occurred to him had it not been for the sagacious intimation of counsel. At the same time He tells Mr. Bradford the sheriff that where he should be executed he wished him to do it? Had he then thought of that apology for his conduct which his more cunning lawyers have since found out. Did he not believe that he had performed an act for which he must render upon his life a sacrifice; and having accomplished the object of his wishes was he not prepared to meet the destiny which awaited him. "Is there I ask any comparison between the declarations of this man and that of Oneby as manifestations of conscious guilt!—as evidences of that malice of mind which is essential to the constitution of murder? If the declaration of Oneby left us doubt of his malice can those of the prisoner be less certain indications? Shall Oneby be pronounced guilty of murder after the fullest and more able trial that ever a subject, and without a depending voice? And shall Magness when guilt is so much more apparent escape unpunished? Oneby had made a threat of vengeance when his passions might have been warm, and when by possibility he might not have any intention to execute it—Magness ills a fellow being and knows the motive of his coward. Oneby no man doubts, was rightfully condemned—but the declarations of the prisoner to Bradford: Drake, Beauford and Phillips which are all uniform—which all tend to the same point—and manifest the existence of malice form a much more unerring proof of guilt. Yes gentlemen, if long experience in the profession has made me acquainted with criminal law, I do say that there cannot exist a plainer, or a stronger case of murder than this. Having said this I think I might now safely confide the cause to your determination. But gentlemen I must own that I feel a remarkable solicitude, for the sake of my country that a stop should be put to the daring inroads of vice which are daily spreading desolation around us. I must therefore beg your indulgence a little longer on this occasion. I wish to explain murder to you in such a way that you cannot mistake its meaning. It is the killing a reasonable creature with malice aforethought? Malice in this case does not mean, as many are to apt to imagine, a principle of malevolence and hatred against particulars—but the term malice meaneth that the fact hath been attended with such circumstances as are the ordinary symptoms of a wicked depraved and malignant spirit (Fort 256). And gentlemen wherever in a charge of murder the fact of killing is proven all the circumstances of accident necessity or infirmity are to be proved by the prisoner unless they arise out of the evidence produced against him; for the law presumeth the fact to be founded in malice till the contrary appeareth (Fort 256). As we have proven the fact of killing it behooves the prisoner if he would escape the conviction of murder to explain away the malice which the fact of killing implies—But instead of being of being able to do this, he has, as we have seen, furnished the strongest additional evidence of the existence of that malice.—If a man strike another with a weapon which is likely to kill it will be murder though no premeditation should be proven. And in this respect our law corresponds with the Divine law. "If a man, says the Bible, strike another with iron so that he die, he shall surely be put to death." The law in this implies malice; for malice may be either express or implied. Then assaults which are spoken of in the books, as justifying or excusing a homicide, and which been read to you so abundantly are not barely attempts to strike—it must be an actual beating.[17]

The record of Whiteside's continuation ends there. It is interesting that he makes reference to the Bible as an alternative source of law. This could be the same set of scriptures that Overton used which the defense attorney's mocked in their presentations to the jury. There are many more legal arguments made by Grundy and Whiteside in the notes of John Reid but they are addressed to the judge as they battled over the language of the jury instructions. While there was no doubt more said than the record shows, the fate of David Magness was placed in the hands of the jury.

17. *Ibid*, 67–69, 70, 82–85.

David Magness's Verdict

It is not known how long the jury deliberated or what questions they asked of the court, but in what must have been a great disappointment to Andrew Jackson and the friends of the Andersons, David was not convicted of murdering Patton Anderson. The jury rendered the following verdict:

> David Magness is not guilty of the murder aforesaid above charged upon him but that the said David Magness is guilty of the felonious slaying of the said Patton Anderson.[18]

In effect, the jury decided that David did not kill Patton Anderson with the malice aforethought that is necessary for murder. The defense had won its case. The jury believed that he was defending his father from the wrathful Anderson.

However, a conviction of the lesser charge of felonious slaying, roughly the equivalent of modern manslaughter, did carry consequences. In rendering his sentence, the court ordered the following penalty:

> The said David Magness be burned in his left hand immediately with the letter "M" and that the said David Magness be imprisoned in the jail of Davidson County there being no sufficient jail in Williamson County for the span of eleven calendar months from this day and that he remain in said jail until he pay all the cost of this prosecution.[19]

The court entered an order instructing the Sheriff of Williamson County to deliver David to the jailer of Davidson County.[20] The judge then issued a separate order remanding Perrygreen Magness and

---

18. Williamson County, Tennessee, Miscellaneous Records 1, 130.
19. *Ibid*, 131.
20. *Ibid*, 132.

Jonathan Magness to the Davidson County Jail "until they shall be brought up for trial at this court at next term."[21]

---

21. *Ibid*, 132.

6

Awaiting Justice in Jail: Perrygreen and Jonathan Magness

The trials of Perrygreen Magness and Jonathan Magness were supposed to begin with the new term of the Fourth Judicial Circuit of Tennessee in May 1811. At the end of David Magness's trial, Perrygreen and Jonathan appealed to the court to provide measures to compel the witnesses to return to the court. The court recorded:

> Upon application of Jonathan and Perry G. Magness—Jacob Hilcham, Archibald Simpson, Isaac Williams, Matthew S. Montgomery, Hugh Barnett, Nicholas Nall, John Perryman, Lewis Newsom, James McQuiston, Gideon Harmon, William Simpson, William Rogers, Harman Newsom, William Newsom, James Gilbert, and John Griffin in open court acknowledge themselves to be indebted to the State of Tennessee

in the sum of two hundred and fifty dollars each to be levied of their personal goods and chattels, lands and tenements but nevertheless to be void on condition that they said shall make their personal appearance before the judge of the fourth circuit at the court house of the county of Williamson on the first Thursday after the second Monday of May next, then and there to give testimony on behalf of said Jonathan Magness and Perry Green Magness on an indictment exhibited against them for the murder of Patton Anderson and not thence depart without leave of the court."[1]

State witnesses were also given orders to return to the court. At the time the Court convened for the May 1811 term, several orders related to witnesses for the Magness trial were issued. An order was entered against Benjamin Bradford "to pay the sum of four hundred dollars to the State of Tennessee for his failing to attend and give testimony at this term against the said Jonathan and Perry Green Magness."[2] George Goodman, William Cunningham, John McCrory, William Mitchell, Robert H Dyer, Samuel Hogg, Joseph Dixen, and Thomas Mitchell who "had been summoned to appear before court on this day and give testimony on behalf of the State against the said defendants Jonathan and Perrygreen Magness" were ordered to "forfeit and pay the sum of one hundred and twenty five dollars each to the State of Tennessee for their non-attendance."[3]

An order was issued against Matthew S. Montgomery to "forfeit and pay to the State two hundred and fifty dollars" for violating his recognizance.[4] David Kies, who was summoned on behalf of Jonathan and Perrygreen, did not appear and was ordered to pay one hundred and twenty five dollars to the State for non-appearance.[5]

Further complicating the court's docket for the May 1811 term was the fact that Jordan Reeves, son-in-law of Jonathan Magness and

1. Williamson County, Tennessee, Miscellaneous Records 1, 132–133.
2. *Ibid*, 203.
3. *Ibid*, 203, 204.
4. *Ibid*, 204, 205.
5. *Ibid*, 206.

chief witness in the defense of his brother-in-law David Magness, was indicted by the grand jury for perjury on May 18, 1811.[6] It appears from the record that the prosecution sought to aggressively punish the key witness and relative of the Magnesses, hoping to taint his testimony and impeach his character for the upcoming trials. The indictment against Reeves, brought in Williamson County by prosecutor Alfred Balch, listed almost every element of his testimony as being false and raised a "who do you believe" scenario.[7] The indictment read as follows:

> Jordan Reeves swore to tell the truth as a witness for David Magness—certain questions were material whether David and Jonathan were in the house of William Newsom in Shelbyville in Bedford County in which Patton Anderson was shot. Whether said Jonathan left the place or said house near the south door where said Anderson first went up to him before the pistol was fired which caused Anderson's death. Whether said Anderson had his hand aiming a blow at Jonathan at the time he was shot, whether Anderson was near enough to said Jonathan to strike him with the dirk in his hand and whether said Jonathan went out of the south or front door of said Newsom house when he left it immediately after said Anderson was shot.[8]

Reeves was accused of contriving to have David Magness acquitted by the Bedford County Grand Jury whose members were: Keeble Terry, John C. Dunn, Andrew Patterson, Hugh McBride, William Locke, Thomas Green, James Walker, James A. Wilson, William Peacock, Lemuel Hutchings, John Byler, Samuel Hughes, Nathan Forrest, James McQuiston, and Edward Cage.[9] Of note,

---

6. State v. Jordan Reeves, Tennessee Divorce, Probate, and Other Records 1800–1899. Williamson County, 1810. Miscellaneous Records (liquor licenses to slave records) Roll B-126: 365.

7. Williamson County, Tennessee, Miscellaneous Records 3, 49.

8. *Ibid.*

9. *Ibid*, 50.

many of these grand jurors had been witnesses for the prosecution in the trial of David Magness.

If the jury believed that Reeves had been untruthful about anything from whether Jonathan Magness "went out the South or the front door" of the Newsom house to whether "Patton Anderson was near enough to said Jonathan Magness to strike him with the dirk," he could go to jail.[10] The perjury trial of Reeves was fundamentally another trial of another member of the Magness family for the murder of Patton Anderson. While there are some original documents concerning this trial, nothing has been found concerning the verdict. As will be discussed later, Reeves was able to post bail for Jonathan and Perrygreen at the end of the May term, suggesting the charges were dropped or he was somehow quickly acquitted.

Despite their chief witness being indicted, the Magnesses offered that they were prepared for their defense.[11] However, the non-appearance of many key witnesses for the State forced the judge to delay the trial of Perrygreen Magness and Jonathan Magness until the next term of the court in November 1811.

Though they would have to wait again for their trials, the judge freed the Magnesses on bond until the next term.[12] In two separate orders, Judge Nathaniel Williamson indebted Jonathan Magness and Perrygreen Magness each with a sum of ten thousand dollars that would be forfeited with their personal appearance in the November court term.[13] He required "good and sufficient security" for the large sums. Certain men pledged to guarantee that Jonathan Magness would appear in court with individual debts to the State of Tennessee of five thousand dollars secured by their "goods and

---

10. State v. Jordan Reeves, Tennessee Divorce, Probate, and Other Records 1800–1899. Williamson County, Tennessee, 1810 Miscellaneous Records (liquor licenses to slave records) Roll B-126: 370-373.

11. Tennessee Legislative Petition 9-1-1812, Petition to the Tennessee Legislature by Jonathan Magness, September 10, 1812.

12. *Ibid.*

13. It is confusing that Judge Nathaniel Williams—who was the judge for the 3rd Circuit—issued these orders. The State of Tennessee passed a law in November 1811 (*Acts of Tennessee of 1811*, Chapter 72) that altered the structure of the Circuit Courts in the state. The law at that time provided that Circuit Judges would rotate circuits in order of the circuit numbers. These orders, however, predate that change.

chattel lands and tenements."[14] Those men were James McQuiston, Jordan Reeves, Simon Bateman, Lewis Newsom, and Isaac Williams. The same men, in addition to James Wills, guarantee that Perrygreen Magness would appear in court by posting five thousand dollars' worth of their goods and chattel lands and tenements as collateral.[15]

While Jonathan was bailed on this indictment until the November term of the court in Williamson County, the judge did note that Magness was "also imprisoned in the jail of Davidson County by virtue of a writ of Capias ad Respondendum at the suit of John C. Hamilton returnable to the court of pleas of Davidson County at their April sessions 1811 as appears by the said Sheriff of Davidson return on said writ of habeas corpus by B Hays attorney of said John C. Hamilton."[16]

November 1811: Perrygreen Gets His Trial

In the November 1811 term, though the judge had ordered bonds for witnesses, the defense of Jonathan Magness was not ready "owing to the absence of some material witnesses."[17]

Upon the application of the Magnesses during the May term, the judge had established financial penalties on the key witnesses to compel their appearance in November. A two hundred and fifty dollar debt to the State of Tennessee was to be voided by the appearance of each of the following: Joel Lewis, Joel D. Harris, John B. Hogg, Samuel Eskridge, Hugh Bennet, John Bradaway, William Bell Jr., Claiborne Williams, Jordan Reeves, William Newsom, Gideon Harmon, Isaac Williams, James McQuiston, Nicholas Nall, Joseph Aike, William Rogers, John McPeak, John Griffin, and William Hale.[18]

---

14. Williamson County, Tennessee Miscellaneous Records 1, 209.
15. *Ibid*.
16. *Ibid*, 211–212.
17. Tennessee Legislative Petition 9-1-1812, Petition to the Tennessee Legislature by Jonathan Magness, September 10, 1812. See also Williamson County, Tennessee Miscellaneous Records Volume 1, 340–341.
18. Williamson County, Tennessee, Miscellaneous Records 1, 207.

Separately, the following witnesses, who were "to give testimony on behalf of the State", were each bonded by two hundred and fifty dollars to appear at the November 1811 term of the court: John Stephens, Edward Ward, John Drake, Malcolm Gilcchrist, John Casey, Samuel Hutchings, Edward Cage, Aaron Gamble, James Alexander, William Tune, John Coffee, Mark Mitchell, Thomas Hicks, Stephen Bedford, John Bradley, and William Nash.[19]

At the start of the November term, Friday, November 15, 1811, a number of witnesses had again failed to appear. The court began the session by ordering John Griffin to forfeit and pay the two hundred and fifty dollars he was indebted for his appearance. John Bradley, William Tune, Benjamin Bradford, Samuel Hogg, and Matthew S. Montgomery were declared delinquent witnesses and ordered to forfeit and pay two hundred and fifty dollars each for non-appearance.[20] Samuel Hogg did eventually appear before the court on November 20, 1811, and was then bonded by another two hundred and fifty dollars to appear at the May term in 1812 to offer testimony against Jonathan Magness.[21]

The Court noted the appearance of Jonathan Magness and Perrygreen Magness and relieved the men who had provided collateral to their bonds from their burden. The ten thousand dollar bail for Jonathan's day-to-day appearance, however, was reimposed.[22]

When the November 1811 session began, Jonathan's defense was not prepared and he was again committed to prison.[23]

The trial of Perrygreen Magness commenced on November 18, 1811. The jurors who would decide his fate were Stephen Barefield, Ruffin Brown, Jessee Tarkinton, Andrew Roundtree, William Banks, James Anderson, Robert McLemore, John Roberts, Joseph Hapell, William Marshall, Richard Hightower, and Matthew Johnson.[24]

---

19. *Ibid*, 207, 208.

20. *Ibid*, 302–305, 310, 317.

21. *Ibid*, 316.

22. *Ibid*, 303, 311.

23. Tennessee Legislative Petition 9-1-1812, Petition to the Tennessee Legislature by Jonathan Magness, September 10, 1812.

24. Williamson County, Tennessee, Miscellaneous Records 1, 312.

On November 19, 1811, Perrygreen filed a petition of habeas corpus for his brother David Magness, who was in the Davidson County jail, to allow him to provide testimony for his defense. The judge granted the motion upon the defense providing security for the costs to the jailer of transporting David to the trial.[25]

In another blow to the friends of Patton Anderson, the jury returned a verdict of not guilty against Perrygreen Magness two days later.[26] The judge also affirmatively decided that Magness would not be "taxed with the costs of the prosecution."[27]

May 1812: Jonathan's Trial

Perrygreen was a free man, but it would not be until the May 1812 term when all the witnesses on both sides were available at court that Jonathan would finally be tried.[28] After Perrygreen's acquittal was entered in November 1811, Judge Stuart bonded the witnesses to appear at the May term of the court to give testimony at Jonathan's trial. The witnesses for the State were John Stephens, John Drake, John McPeak, Joseph Alexander, Aaron Gambell, Benjamin Bradford, Malcolm Gilchrist, John Casey, Edward Ward, Thomas Mitchell, William Nash, and Stephen Bedford.[29] Witnesses for the defense were John Broadway, Nicholas Null, William Rogers, Joseph Ake, Joel D. Harris, John McPeak, Isaac Williams, Samuel Hutchings, Claiborn Williams, William Hall, Thomas Hicks, James Gilbert, Joel Lewis, William Bell Jr., Archibald Simpson, Jordan Reeves, Hugh Barnett, William Newsom, Lewis Newsom, William Simpson, Matthew S. Montgomery, James McQuiston, John Stephens, and Gideon Harmon.[30]

Jonathan Magness petitioned the court for a special session and the court agreed to convene itself again on the fifth Monday of

---

25. *Ibid*, 314.
26. *Ibid*, 320.
27. *Ibid*, 321.
28. Tennessee Legislative Petition 9-1-1812, Petition to the Tennessee Legislature by Jonathan Magness, September 10, 1812.
29. Williamson County, Tennessee Miscellaneous Records 1, 321.
30. *Ibid*, 322.

December 1811. On December 31, Jonathan petitioned for the release of his son David Magness from the Davidson County jail so that he might testify on his behalf.[31] The record of this short session does not show any action taken by either the prosecution or defense. On January 1, 1812, the court ordered that Jonathan Magness would be charged with the costs of that session and bonded the regular witnesses to appear for a term of the court in March 1812.[32] Jonathan Magness was "again committed to prison."[33]

No action or matter regarding or related to the Magnesses appear in the court records until the next regular session of the court in May 1812. The May term of the Fourth Circuit Court was presided over by Judge Nathaniel Williams of the Third Circuit.

On May 13, Judge Williams ordered that Jonathan Magness be released from the Davidson County jail and presented for trial in Williamson County.[34] The trial began on May 15, 1812, and lasted until May 22, 1812. The jurors in the case were Jessee White, William Anthony, Thomas Old, John Edmondson, James Bradley, John D. Hill, James Morret, Newton Cannon, Thomas Miles, William Nolen, Richard Hughes, and Sion Hunt.[35] During the trial, a constable named Samuel Andrews was fined twenty-five dollars "for his contempt of this court in not attending said jury as he was ordered."[36]

The trial largely centered on whether there was a conspiracy by the Magnesses to kill Anderson, or if the conflict and shooting were spontaneous. There is a great deal of legal back and forth in the record, but ultimately the question that was presented to the jury was as follows: "Can a conspiracy take into account a drunk Anderson starting a fight?"[37] In other words, could the defendants rely on the

---

31. *Ibid*, 349.

32. *Ibid*, 350, 351.

33. Tennessee Legislative Petition 9-1-1812, Petition to the Tennessee Legislature by Jonathan Magness, September 10, 1812. See also Williamson County, Tennessee ,Miscellaneous Records 1, 340, 341.

34. Williamson County, Tennessee, Miscellaneous Records 1, 377

35. *Ibid*, 386.

36. *Ibid*, 402.

37. Reid, 145.

person they wanted to kill in their conspiracy to start a fight and wield a deadly weapon?

In yet another loss for the friends of Anderson, on May 22, 1812, the jury returned a verdict of not guilty in favor of Jonathan Magness.[38] However, the Anderson cabal would have a certain degree of vengeance. After the verdict, the prosecution moved the court to tax Jonathan Magness with the costs of the prosecution.[39] The defense filed a "bill of exception" on this point but nonetheless Jonathan Magness was remanded to jail "which was done accordingly."[40]

It seems Andrew Jackson continued to follow closely and attend the trials of the Magnesses. Newton Cannon, one of the jurors in Jonathan's trial who would later serve in Congress and as governor of Tennessee, is prominent in stories about the trial because of his interaction with the General after the acquittal.[41] Many of them claim Jackson was "shaking his fist at the nose" of one of the jurors after David Magness's trial, but the most accurate recounting is given by historian James Phelan:

> [Newton Cannon] was on the jury that tried Magness, the father of the man who shot Patton Anderson. Jackson, a warm and enthusiastic friend of Anderson, spared no exertion to have Magness convicted. He was acquitted. Jackson shook his finger in the face of the obstinate young juror and said, "I'll mark you, young man."[42]

For all his anger with the jury, Jackson must have been very pleased with the judges of the Fourth Judicial Circuit. While a jury had acquitted Jonathan Magness and his son David had served his eleven-month jail sentence, both men remained in jail.

---

38. Williamson County, Tennessee, Miscellaneous Records 1, 405.

39. Ibid.

40. Ibid, 406.

41. Robert V. Remini, *Andrew Jackson and the Course of American Empire, 1767–1821*. New York: Harper and Row, 1977, 162. See also Burke Davis, *Old Hickory: A Life of Andrew Jackson*. New York: The Dial Press, New York, 63.

42. James Phelan, *History of Tennessee: The Making of a State*. Boston and New York: Houghton, Mifflin, and Company, 1888, 359.

A motion appearing to be an appeal to the trial court was considered, but the judge explained that he "fully understood" and verified that the defendant, though found not guilty, was to be "committed" until he could pay "the costs of the present prosecution."[43] Another bill of exception was seemingly filed "on the matter to tax the defendant with the costs of the prosecution in this case."[44] Magness again took exception to the Court's opinion and his objections were "signed and sealed and ordered to be made a part of the record."[45]

In his penultimate order of the term, Judge Nathaniel Williams directed the Williamson County sheriff to remand Jonathan Magness to the jail of Davidson County.[46] In his final order of the term, he ordered that David Magness join his father there.[47] Though their lawyers had soundly defeated the Anderson-Jackson legal team, the Magnesses were nonetheless sitting in jail with no foreseeable way out.

---

43. Williamson County, Tennessee, Miscellaneous Records 1, 411.
44. *Ibid*, 413.
45. *Ibid*.
46. *Ibid*, 414.
47. *Ibid*.

Aftermath of the Trials

Found not guilty, Jonathan Magness nonetheless languished in the Nashville jail. The same fate befell his brother David even though he had served his eleven-month sentence. David's sentence and Jonathan's order of acquittal required them to pay some $800 in court costs, but neither could do so.[1]

The brothers applied to the Circuit Court to be discharged under the law for the relief of insolvent debtors.[2] The court, however, was given testimony that they were not insolvent. On May 23, 1812, the prosecutors of Jonathan Magness complained to the court that he was hiding property and entered into the record the sworn testimony of Hinchey Pettway, who claimed "the son of the defendant carried

---

1. Petition of David Magness, Tennessee Legislative Petitions 9-1-1812.

2. Petition of Jonathan Magness, Tennessee Legislative Petitions 9-1-1812, and Petition of David Magness, Tennessee Legislative Petitions 9-1-1812.

nine or ten negroes of the defendant's property towards Missouri where the process of law could not reach them."³ At this point in the court record, the phrase "the Indian Nations" was marked through and replaced with "Missouri." In May 1812, the Louisiana Territory was in the process of being named the Missouri Territory to avoid confusion after the State of Louisiana, formerly the Territory of Orleans, had entered the Union in April 1812. The Missouri Territory would not be officially created until June 4, 1812.⁴

The Magnesses Relocate to Arkansas before May 23, 1812

The Magnesses's original motions to be released under the insolvency laws were rejected. Now they faced the prospect of "perpetual imprisonment."⁵ In the notes of John Reid, there is a great deal of legal discussion about the treatment of insolvent debtors.⁶ These papers appear to have been prepared for arguments before the court on the scope of the law and whether it applied to the types of debt the Magnesses owed and whether they could, in fact, receive relief under the law.⁷ However, in the spring of 1812, the court seemed more focused on the questions of fact in the case and whether the Magnesses were stashing property across the Mississippi River so they could claim insolvency.

On September 10, 1812, both Jonathan Magness and his son David petitioned the Tennessee Legislature to release them. Jonathan's petition read:

---

3. Tennessee Divorce, Probate, and Other Records, 1800–1899, Tennessee County Records, Tennessee State Library and Archives, Nashville, TN. Williamson County, 1810 Miscellaneous Records (liquor licenses to slave records) Roll B-126, 332. History would prove the prosecution correct. It was a young Morgan Magness, younger brother of David and Perrygreen, who was shepherding the Magness family's property and wealth out of the State of Tennessee during the incarceration of his father and brother.

4. "An Act providing for the government of the territory of Missouri," United States Statutes at Large, Twelfth Congress, Session I, Chapter 95, June 4, 1812.

5. Petition of Jonathan Magness, Tennessee Legislative Petition # 9-1-1812, and Petition of David Magness, Tennessee Legislative Petitions #9-1-1812.

6. Reid, 125–128.

7. *Ibid.*

To the Honorable the General Assembly of the state of Tennessee

The petition of Jonathan Magness humbly sheweth

That in the month of October 1810 he was indicted by the grand jury in the Circuit Court for the County of Bedford for the murder of Patton Anderson and was immediately committed to prison. The case was removed for trial to the Circuit Court for the County of Williamson; and November term of that court 1810 your petitioner was ready for his trial and was not tried but committed again to prison. In may term 1811 he was again ready for his trial and the State not being ready he was bailed: In November term 1811 your petitioner was not ready owing to the absence of some material witnesses and was again committed to prison. In May Term 1812 your petitioner was tried when all the witnesses on both sides were found and was acquitted without the least hesitation on the part of the jury. The nature of the evidence and its utter incompetency to affect a conviction, can be stated by one of the members of your Honorable body who was one of the jury.

Your petitioner was then committed for costs and is unable to pay them and must suffer imprisonment for life unless he can be allowed the benefit of the insolvent debtors act. And that benefit hath lately been denied to others, in the circumstances by the Circuit Court; the Court conceiving that the act did not extend to one imprisoned for costs on Criminal prosecution.

Your petitioner hath now suffered imprisonment for eighteen months and more—He has been declared innocent by a respectable jury of his fellow citizens—his health is impaired—His fortune is ruined by the neglect of his affairs and the advantaged taken of his situation; and his family have been plunged into the deepest distress.

In vain has your petitioner looked to our mild Constitution which forbids unusual punishments and orders a discharge from imprisonment in case of insolvency. In vain has he expected relief from the laws in being. He is told from authority that no law in being will afford him relief. Others before him have been imprisoned for costs in Criminal cases and though unable to pay them have not suffered perpetual imprisonment—yet it cannot be ascertained under what law they have been released so as to make their cases precedents for that of your petitioner. Your Honorable Body as guardians of the rights of your fellow citizens cannot be indifferent to the unjust sufferings of one, however humble may be his condition—Nor can you be regardless of any unconstitutional means which may be resorted to for the infliction of punishment, which the law will not inflict, nor our Constitution endure.

Under your protection therefore your petitioner desires to take refuge. And to seek for relief against oppression.

May it therefore please you Honorable body to call upon Colonel Cannon and the jailer in Nashville for the verification of these facts and to provide such relief for your petitioner as his case may seem to require.

Jonathan Magness maketh oath that the facts above stated are true to the best of his knowledge and belief and particularly the fact of his insolvency—for that he is not worth ten dollars in any worldly substance—it is true, he saith, that he hath been in possession of property since the commencement of his imprisonment to a large amount but that the same hath been swept away by executions obtained for the most part against his estate, since his imprisonment. And he saith further that he hath not conveyed away any of his property with intent to defraud any of his creditors to whom he is indebted.

N.B. The said Jonathan Magness (unreadable word) to the words of not being worth ten dollars, but is perfectly willing to give up to the law and the proper authority thereof the whole amo[unt] of property now in his hands.

Sworn to subscribed before us this 9th Sept 1812.
Tho. Gillahunty
Thomas Williamson JP   Jonathan Magness[8]

David's petition reads:

---

8. Petition of Jonathan Magness, Tennessee Legislative Petition 9-1-1812.

To the Honorable the General Assembly of the State of Tennessee

The petition of David Magness humbly sheweth.

That in November term of the Circuit Court for the County of Williamson in the 1810 he was tried upon and Indictment found against himself and Jonathan Magness, and Peregrine Magness for the murder of Patton Anderson and was found guilty of manslaughter. And your petitioner was sentenced to eleven months imprisonment and until the costs of the prosecution were paid. The eleven months expired in October 1811. And your petitioner being really insolvent and unable to pay the costs which amount to the sum of eight hundred dollars and more, has been ever since confined in jail. No attempt has been made to hire out your petitioner under the Act of 1787 Ch. 14. The officer no doubt being satisfied that no person could be found who would pay that sum for him. Your petitioner hath applied to the Circuit Court for the County of Davidson, and also to the Circuit Court for the County of Williamson to be discharged under the law for the relief of insolvent debtors, or under any other law which would sanction the proceeding. His application in both instances has been rejected and now no expectation remains but that of perpetual imprisonment unless your Honorable body will interpose and save him from it. It is a punishment incompatible with the principles of a free government. It is forbidden by our Constitution Sec 16 and 18 of the Bill of rights. And indeed the sentence itself above referred to, tho' allowed by an ancient English Statute, is unprecedented in this Country, and is certainly discountenanced, if not repealed, by the true spirit of our republican institutions.

Your petitioner by way of prompting the attention of your Honorable Body to the peculiar hardships of his case would beg leave humbly to ask what has become of all those who have heretofore been imprisoned for costs in Criminal cases and have been unable to pay them? Are they yet in prison? And why ate the unfortunate more severely treated at this time than formerly? It is impossible that those who are selected to see the Constitution preserved—its principles fostered and grievances of all sorts removed from the Citizen, can behold without some emotion a case of the complexion of that which is now presented to them.

Your petitioner is animated with the only hope now left him that the representatives of free men will never endure the adoption into our system of a mode of punishment which is the worst times of the most despotic governments hath ever been deemed the most odious engine of tyranny.

And your petitioner humbly prays your Honors to do some act for his relief which will enable him once more to see his friends; resume his occupations; and to be released from his present abode of misery.

Sworn to and subscribed before me this 9th Sept. 1812
Tho. Gillihunty
Thomas Williamson JP   David Magness[9]

Magnesses Released From Jail

Jonathan Magness was finally released from jail on November 2, 1812. He wasn't released by specific action or private bill of the state legislature, but rather by virtue of an "insolvent law" passed by the Tennessee General Assembly. Edward D. Hobbs, the jailer of Davidson County, explained the nature of Jonathan's release and included a copy of the court order, in a petition to the Tennessee legislature asking to be remunerated for the costs of jailing Jonathan Magness.

In the petition, dated June 3, 1813, Hobbs hoped he could be reimbursed for having jailed Jonathan Magness "until he was discharged under the insolvent law passed at the last session of the General Assembly."[10] This Act provided for the discharge of insolvent prisoners and apparently also for the "payment of jailers fees when prisoners are discharged by a judge." Hobbs noted that he had held Jonathan Magness in jail, with "exception for the different periods

9. Petition of David Magness, Tennessee Legislative Petition 9-1-1812.

10. Petition of Edward Hobbs, Tennessee Legislative Petitions Roll #4, Petition #6, Session 3, 1813, June 3, 1813.

when he was taken out for trial" from "on or about the 29th day of October 1810" until "the 2nd of November, 1812."[11]

The terms of David Magness's release are less well documented. What provided for his release may not have been an Act of the Tennessee legislature, but rather indirectly, by Acts of Congress. In two separate Acts, one in February 1812 and another in July 1812, Congress authorized the president to accept the services of fifty thousand volunteers for service in the war that was brewing against Great Britain. The gathering of this army was the vehicle by which an ambitious Andrew Jackson would propel himself from obscurity.[12]

As commanding officer of the Tennessee militia, Jackson received orders in November 1812 to quickly gather the army Congress had authorized. Coincidentally, both Jonathan and David Magness were added to the list of men eligible for the Davidson County Militia in 1812. Because these roles were also the voter rolls, assuredly the Magnesses were added after Jonathan Magness was released from jail on November 2, 1812. Notably theirs are two of the last three names added to a list of 1,114 men eligible for the militia and the vote in Davidson County.[13]

While Jonathan was released specifically under the insolvent debtor laws, poorly documented stories and family legends claim that David Magness was released from jail in order to provide Jackson with troops he desperate needed. No documentary evidence of this has been found. David did serve under Jackson in the Creek War and at New Orleans in the War of 1812.[14] Further, early Jackson biographers noted that in times when his "requisition was not complete, wither in the number of men, or the necessary equipment," that Jackson would order measures be "instantly taken to remedy the deficiency."[15] It is logical to assume that one measure Jackson

---

11. *Ibid.*

12. John Reid and John Henry Eaton, *The Life of Andrew Jackson*. Samuel Bradford Publisher, 1824, 18.

13. Edythe Rucker Whitley, *Pioneers of Davidson County, Tennessee*. Baltimore: Genealogical Publishing Company, Inc., 1979, 25.

14. Josiah H Shinn, *Pioneers and Makers of Arkansas*, Washington, D.C.: Genealogical and Historical Publishing Company, 1908, 162.

15. Reid and Eaton, *Life of Andrew Jackson*, 36.

The testimony of H. Pettiway stating that Jonathan Magness was not insolvent as he claimed. This turned out to be true.
(Tennessee Divorce, Probate, and Other Records, 332)

may have used to fill his ranks was the release of vigorous prisoners who could potentially provide their own horses and supplies.

After a two-year ordeal of jail and legal troubles, all of the Magnesses were free from jail and no doubt eager to leave Tennessee. David and Jordan Reeves were at war, but Perrygreen, Jonathan, and family members who remained in Tennessee in 1812 soon headed west to join who had ventured into a new land.

The prosecutors had been correct in May when they suggested that one of Jonathan Magness's sons had been hiding property in the Missouri Territory. His sixteen-year-old son Morgan had in fact escaped with the family's property and established himself on the White River in what would become Arkansas. Jonathan, Perrygreen, and David quickly joined him in Arkansas. Morgan's other brothers, William and John, eventually settled there with large families. His sisters Mary (Magness) Reeves and Sarah (Magness) Bateman, his half-sister Mary Ann, his cousin James, and his uncles Robert and Samuel—the brothers of Jonathan—would all flee Tennessee for Arkansas as well.

The story of the Magness trials of Tennessee provides a window to the violence and rugged justice of the early American frontier. The trials themselves were a turning point in the lives of almost all its participants. Felix Grundy, Andrew Jackson, and Thomas Hart Benton began their soaring ascents in American politics and became important men in American history. The Magness family escaped their ignominy in Tennessee and became "one of the most respectable and extensive in the [Arkansas] territory."[16]

16. C.F.M. Noland, "Early Times in Arkansas," *Arkansas State Gazette and Democrat*, January 9, 1858.

Bibliography

Manuscripts and Court Documents

Bedford County, Virginia, Court Order Book 3 (February 1765). Bedford County Circuit Court Clerk, Bedford, VA.

Biographical file of Senator Jenkin Whiteside. Notes of A.P. Foster, Assistant Librarian and Archivist, State of Tennessee Department of Education, Division of Library and Archives transmitted to the Congress of the United States, Joint Committee on Printing (March 1926). U.S. Senate Historian's Office, Washington, DC.

Dyas Collection of the John Coffee Papers 17701917. Tennessee State Library and Archives, Research Department, Nashville, TN.

Early Tennessee General Land Grants, Roll 28, Book D (March 1811). Tennessee State Library and Archives, Research Department, Nashville, TN.

John Reid papers, 1802–1842. MMC-3365, Manuscript Division, Library of Congress, Washington, DC.

Prince George's County, Maryland Deed Books Q, NN, and RR. Prince George's County Clerk of the Circuit Court, Land Records Division, Upper Marlboro, MD.

Tennessee Divorce, Probate, and Other Records 1800–1899. Tennessee County Records, Williamson County, 1810, Miscellaneous Records (liquor licenses to slave records). Tennessee State Library and Archives, Research Department, Nashville, TN.

Tennessee Legislative Petitions 1799–1850. Tennessee State Library and Archives, Research Department, Nashville, TN.

Tryon County, North Carolina, Deed Book 1. Tryon County Record of Deeds (filed with Lincoln County 1768-1779). State Archives of North Carolina, Raleigh, NC.

Wilson County, Tennessee, Deed Books B and C. Wilson County Tennessee Register of Deeds, Lebanon, TN.

Newspapers

Arkansas Gazette, September 16, 1871.
Nashville Democratic Clarion, November 2, 1810.

Published Works, Dissertations, and Theses

Anderson, James D. *Making the American Thoroughbred; Especially in Tennessee, 1800–1845*. Norwood, Mass: Plimpton Press, 1916. Reprinted Memphis: General Books, 2010.

Balch, Thomas Willing. *Balch Genealogica*. Philadelphia: Allen, Lane, and Scott, 1907.

Bassett, John Spencer. *Correspondence of Andrew Jackson* I. Washington, DC: Carnegie Institution, 1926.

Baylor, Orval W. "The Career of Felix Grundy, 1777–1840. An Address Before the Filson Club February 2, 1942." *The Filson Club Quarterly* 16: 2 (April 1942).

Benton, Thomas H. *Thirty Years View*. New York: Greenwood Press Publishers, 1968.

Burstein, Andrew. *The Passions of Andrew Jackson*. New York: Vintage Books, 2004.

Chambers, William N. "Thomas Hart Benton in Tennessee." *Tennessee Historical Quarterly* 8:4 (December 1949).

Chambers, William Nisbet. *Old Bullion Benton, Senator from the New West: Thomas Hart Benton, 1782–1858*. Boston: Little Brown and Co., 1956.

Cheatham, Mark R. *Andrew Jackson Southerner*. Baton Rouge: Louisiana State University Press, 2013.

Corlew, Robert Ewing. *Tennessee: A Short History*. Knoxville: The University of Tennessee Press, 1990.

Cowdon, John B. *Tennessee's Celebrated Case*. Published by author, 1958.

Crutchfield, James A. and Holladay, Robert. *Franklin: Tennessee's Handsomest Town*. Franklin, TN: Hillsboro Press, 1999.

Davis, Burke. *Old Hickory: A Life of Andrew Jackson*. New York: The Dial Press, 1977.

Drake, Francis S. *Dictionary of American Biography*. Boston: Houghton Osgood and Company, 1879.

Ewing, Frances Howard. "The Senatorial Career of the Hon. Felix Grundy." *Tennessee Historical Magazine*, 2d Ser. 2 (October 1931), 3–27; (January 1932) 111–135; (April 1932) 220–224; (July 1932) 270–291.

Foote, Henry S. *The Bench and Bar of the South and Southwest*. St. Louis: Soule, Thomas and Wentworth, 1876.

Griffin, Clarence W. *History of Old Tryon and Rutherford Counties, North Carolina, 1730–1936*. Ashville: Miller Printing Company, 1937.

Guild, Josephus Conn. *Old Times in Tennessee: Historical, Personal, and Political Scraps and Sketches*. Nashville, TN: Tavel, Eastman, and Howell, 1878.

Hale, Will T. and Merritt, Dixon L. *A History of Tennessee and Tennesseans* 3. Chicago and New York: The Lewis Publishing Company, 1913.

Haywood, John. *Civil and Political History of Tennessee*. Nashville: Publishing House of the Methodist Episcopal Church, South, 1891.

Heiskell, S.G. *Andrew Jackson and Early Tennessee History*. Nashville: Ambrose Printing Company, 1918.

Heller, J. Roderick III. *Democracy's Lawyer: Felix Grundy of the Old Southwest*. Baton Rouge, Louisiana State University Press, 2010.

James, Marquis. *Andrew Jackson: The Border Captain*. New York: Grosset and Dunlap, 1933.

Johnson, Patricia Givens. "William P. Anderson and 'The May Letters,'" *Filson Club History Quarterly* 47:2 (April 1973), 174.

Kennedy, John F. *Profiles in Courage–Memorial Edition*. New York: Harper and Row, 1964.

Lynch, Louise Gillespie. *Williamson County, Tennessee, Miscellaneous Records* Volumes 1 and 3. Franklin, TN: Published by author, 1980.

Manley, Walter W. *The Supreme Court of Florida and Its Predecessor Courts 1821–1917*. Gainesville: University of Florida Press, 1997.

McKellar, Kenneth. *Tennessee Senators As Seen By One Of Their Successors*. Kingsport, TN: Southern Publishers, Inc., 1942.

Meigs, William Montgomery. *The Life of Thomas Hart Benton*. Philadelphia: J.B. Lippincott Company, 1904.

Miller, Charles A. *Official and Political Manual of the State of Tennessee*. Nashville: Marshall and Bruce Stationers, 1890.

Moore, John T. *Tennessee, The Volunteer State 1769–1923* 2. Nashville: S.J. Clarke Publishing Company, 1923.

Moser, Harold D., Sharon Macpherson, Charles F. Bryan Jr., eds. *The Papers of Andrew Jackson* 2 (1829). Knoxville: University of Tennessee Press, 2007.

Noland, C.F.M. *Early Times in Arkansas*. Little Rock: *Arkansas State Gazette and Democrat*, January 9, 1858.

"Papers of the First Council of Safety of the Revolutionary Party in South Carolina, June-November, 1775." *The South Carolina Historical and Genealogical Magazine* 1:2 (April, 1900).

Parks, Joseph Howard. *Felix Grundy: Champion of Democracy*. Baton Rouge: Louisiana State University Press, 1940.

Parton, James. *Life of Andrew Jackson in Three Volumes*. New York: Mason Brothers, 1861.

Phelan, James. *History of Tennessee: The Making of a State*. Boston and New York: Houghton, Mifflin, and Company, 1888.

Pitts, Judge John A. *Personal and Professional Reminiscences of an Old Lawyer*. Kingsport, TN: Southern Publishers, Inc., 1930.

Powell, William S. *Dictionary of North Carolina Biography* 2, D-G. Chapel Hill: University of North Carolina Press, 1979.

Ratner, Lorman A. *Andrew Jackson and His Tennessee Lieutenants*. Westport, CT: Greenwood Press, 1997.

Reid, John and John Henry Eaton. *The Life of Andrew Jackson*. Philadelphia: Samuel Bradford Publisher, 1824.

Remini, Robert V. *Andrew Jackson and the Course of American Empire, 1767–1821*. New York: Harper and Row Publishers, 1977.

Roosevelt, Theodore. *Thomas Hart Benton*. Boston and New York: Houghton Mifflin and Company, 1886.

Roster of Soldiers from North Carolina in the American Revolution. Durham, N.C: North Carolina Daughters of the American Revolution, 1932.

Saunders, William L. *Minutes of the Tryon County Committee of Safety, Tryon County (N.C.). Committee of Safety, January 23, 1776–January 24, 1776. Colonial and State Records of North Carolina* 10. Raleigh: F.M. Hale Printer for the State, 1886.

Shinn, Josiah H. *Pioneers and Makers of Arkansas*. Washington, D.C.: Genealogical and Historical Publishing Company, 1908.

Skinner, Vernon L. *Abstracts of the Testamentary Proceedings of the Prerogative Court of Maryland* 19–27. Baltimore: Clearfield Company, 2008.

Speed, Thomas. *The Political Club*. Louisville: John P. Morton and Company, 1894.

Stubblefield, Jeanette. *Another Chapter of "Peregren's Progeny"—Direct Lineage of Benjamine Magness, Son of Jonathan*. Published by author, 1988.

U.S. Congress. *Biographical Directory of the United States Congress, 1774–2005*. House of Representatives Document 108-222. One-Hundred-and-Eighth Congress, Second Session. Washington: U.S. Government Printing Office. 2005.

U.S. Congress. House of Representatives Report C.C.—No. 263, Report of the U.S. Court of Claims to the House of Representatives Re: C.J. Jenkins and W.W. Mann, Assignees of John McKinnie. Thirty-Sixth Congress, Second Session, 1860–1861 (December 18, 1860).

U.S. Congress. *Congressional Globe*, Twenty-Sixth Congress, Second Session, Volume 9 (1841).

U.S. Congress. House of Representatives, Executive Doc. No. 452. Twenty-fifth Congress, Second Session (July 3, 1838).

Watson, Thomas E. *The Life and Times of Andrew Jackson*. Thomson, GA: The Jeffersonian Publishing Company, 1912.

Webb, Gary Alan. "The Magness Trials." *Williamson County Historical Journal* 15 (1984).

Webb, Thomas G. *Early Virginia Families with Tennessee Connections*. Smithville, TN: Bradley Printing Company, 2009

Webb, Thomas G. *The Webb Families of DeKalb County, Tennessee and 23 Related Families*. Smithville, TN: Bradley Printing Company, 2002.

Whitley, Edythe Rucker. *Pioneers of Davidson County, Tennessee.* Baltimore: Genealogical Publishing Company, Inc., 1979.

Williams, Emma Inman. *Historic Madison: The Story of Jackson and Madison County, Tennessee from Mound Builders to World War I.* Jackson, TN: McCowat-Mercer Press, 1946.

Index

A

Acts of Congress, 119
Aike, Joseph, 105, 107
Alexander, James, 106
Alexander, Joseph, 63, 107
Anderson-Jackson legal team, 110
Anderson, Patton (Major) 3, 4, 5, 6, 7, 8, 9, 10, 11, 12, 22, 38, 49, 50, 51, 52, 53, 54, 56, 57, 59, 60, 61, 64, 65, 68, 69, 71, 72, 73, 75, 76, 77, 78, 81, 82, 83, 86, 91, 93, 94, 99, 102, 103, 104, 107, 108, 109, 113, 115
Anderson, Col. William Preston, 4, 10f, 11, 12, 22, 23, 60, 63

Andrews, Samuel, 108
Anthony, William, 108
Avery, Waightstill, 6

B

Balch, Alfred (Fourth Circuit Solicitor General), 9, 15, 37, 38, 39, 40, 103
Bank of the United States, 36
Banks, William, 106
Bardstown, KY, 16
Barefield, Stephen, 106
Barnett, Hugh, 62, 101, 107
Bateman, Sarah (Magness), 118
Bateman, Simon, 105
Battle of Cowpens, 44

Baylor, Orval, 19
Beaufort, Mr., 97
Bedford County Courthouse, 8, 9, 88
Bedford County, TN, 8, 10, 11, 33, 37, 53, 55, 68, 71, 103, 113
Bedford County, VA, 43
Bedford, Stephen, 12, 55, 91, 106, 107
Bell, William Jr., 105, 107
Bennet, Hugh, 105
Benton, Ann (Gooch), 30
Benton, Jesse (brother of Thomas Hart Benton), 34
Benton, Jesse (father of Thomas Hart Benton), 30
Benton, Thomas Hart, 11, 15, 30, 31, 32, 33, 34, 35, 36, 37, 38, 65, 119
Berkeley County, VA, 16
Berry, Thomas, 50
Big Hickory Creek (Tyron County, NC), 44
Bowling Green, KY, 46
Bradaway, John, 105
Bradford, Benjamin, 12, 56, 68, 92, 97, 102, 106, 107
Bradley, James, 108
Bradley, John, 12, 106
Bradley, Major, 64
British Parliament, 43
Britton, Richard, 64
Broadway, John, 107
Broadway, Joseph, 64
Broadway's, 58
Brown, Ruffin, 106
Brownsville, PA, 16
Brushy Creek (Rutherford County, NC), 44
Buffalo Creek, NC, 43
Burke County, NC, 45
Butler, Lydia, 23
Butler, Dr. William E., 23
Byler, John, 103

C

Cage, Edward, 12, 62, 103, 106
Calhoun, John C., 37
Callaway, James, 43
Cannon, Colonel, 114
Cannon, Newton, 108, 109
Carroll, William, 34
Casey, John (Bedford County Prosecutor), 10
Casey, John (witness in Magness trial), 14, 53, 54, 55, 56, 57, 63, 69, 70, 86, 87, 106, 107
Catawba River (NC), 43
Chambers, William, 33, 65
Chickasaw Bluff, 28
Clay, Henry, 16
Cleveland County, NC, 43
Coffee, John, 11, 12, 13, 14, 106
Coleman, Joseph, Esq., 64
Collingsworth, James, 39
Colyar, Col. A.S., 19
Compromise of 1850, 36
Cook, Henry, 50
Cowden, John B., 45f
Creek Indians, 39
Creek War, 117
Creitcher, Mr., 12
Cunningham, William, 102

D

Davidson County Jail, 4
Davidson County, TN, 15, 46, 47, 99, 100, 105, 107, 115, 117
Davis, Nicholas, 43
Declaration of Independence, 43
Dement, Cader, 64
Democratic Clarion (Nashville), 8
Dickinson, Charles, 7
Dickson County, TN, 33
Dixen, Joseph, 102

INDEX

Donelson, John, 28
Donelson, Rachel, 28
Drake, John, 12, 14, 51, 56, 57, 68, 80, 82, 91, 94, 97, 106, 107
Duck River (TN), 59
Dunn, John C., 103
Dunn, Michael C. (Davidson County Sheriff), 14
Durham, Polly, 45
Dyer, Robert H., 102

E

Eaton, John, 12, 12f,
Eaton, John H., 18, 58
Edmondson, John, 108
Eskridge, Mr., 52, 56, 70, 71, 91
Eskridge, Samuel, 56, 105

F

Fairfax County, VA, 42
Fielder, John L., 50
Fisher's case, 80
Fletcher family, 47
Florida, Middle District of, 40
Foote, Henry, 24
Forrest, Nathan, 103
Foster, Ephraim, 18
Fourth District Circuit Court of Tennessee, 8, 14, 37, 101, 108, 109
Fourth District Circuit Court Solicitor General, 9, 15, 37
Franklin, TN, 3, 11, 14, 15, 23, 30, 49

G

Gaines, Thomas, 42
Gamble (Gambell), Aaron, 106, 107
Georgetown, District of Columbia, 37
Gideon, James, 50

Gilbert, James, 60, 101, 107
Gilchrist, Malcolm "Mal," 12, 56, 106, 107
Giles County, TN, 33
Gillahunty, Thomas, 114
Glasgow, James, 20
Glower, Mr. (murder victim in the Oneby case), 95
Goff, Andrew, 50
Goodman, George, 102
Gower (murder victim), 96
Graham, Col. William, 44
Green, Thomas, 103
Griffin, John, 12, 58, 59, 101, 105, 106
Griffin, William, 88, 91
Grundy, Felix, 15, 16, 17, 18, 19, 22, 24, 26, 33, 51, 65, 67, 74, 81, 98, 119
Guild, Judge Josephus, 18, 19, 23, 24
Gwinn, Ransom, 64

H

Hale, William, 105
Hale's Pleas of the Crown, 76
Halifax County, NC, 19
Hall, Mr., 60
Hall, William, 107
Hamilton, John C., 105
Hamilton, William, 12, 14
Hamrick, Sarah, 42
Hapell, Joseph, 106
Harmon (Harman), Gideon, 60, 101, 105, 107
Harris, Joel D., 105, 107
Hartgrove, James, 50
Hart's Hill, 30
Hayes, 23
Hayes, O.B., 15, 24
Hays, 22, 23
Hays, Andrew, 15, 23, 24
Hays, B., 105

Hays, Patsy, 23
Hays, Stockley Donelson, 15, 23
Haywood, Egbert, 19
Haywood, John, 15, 20, 21, 22, 33, 67, 70, 74, 94
Haywood's *The Christian Advocate*, 20
Haywood's *Justice* (treatise), 20
Haywood's *The Civil and Political History of Tennessee*, 20
Haywood's *The Natural and Aboriginal History of Tennessee*, 20
Hermitage, The (home of Andrew Jackson), 34, 46
Hickman County, TN, 33
Hickory Creek (NC), 43
Hicks, James, 50
Hicks, Mr., 64
Hicks, Thomas, 106, 107
Hightower, Richard, 106
Hilcham, Jacob, 101
Hillsborough, NC, 30
Hobbs, Edward D. (Davidson County Jailer), 116
Hogg, Dr. Samuel, 102, 106
Hogg, John B., 58, 105
Holland, Kemp, 50
Hughes, Richard, 108
Hughes, Samuel, 103
Hulme, William (Williamson County Sheriff), 14
Hunt, Sion, 108
Hutchings, John, 12
Hutchings, Lemmel, 12
Hutchings, Samuel, 106, 107
Hutchins, Lemuel, 58, 103

I

Indian Nations, 112
Indiana Territory, 46

J

Jackson, Andrew, 3, 4, 5, 6, 7, 10f, 11, 12, 12f, 13, 22, 23, 27, 28, 30, 33, 34, 35, 36, 38, 48, 49, 63, 64, 65, 99, 109, 117, 119
Jackson, Rachel, 23
Jackson Papers, The, 49
James, Marquis, 49
Johnson, Matthew, 106
Johnson, Mr., 12
Jonesborough, TN, 6

K

Kavanaugh, Doctor, 60
Kennedy, Senator John F., 36
Kentucky Constitutional Convention, 16
Kentucky House of Representatives, 16
Kentucky Supreme Court of Errors and Appeals, 16
Kershaw, Captain Eli, 44
Kershaw's Company, Thompson's Regiment, South Carolina Rangers, 44
Kies, David, 102
King George III (Great Britain), 43
King vs. Cooper case, 77
Knob Creek (North Carolina), 43
Knoxville, TN, 26

L

Lafferty family, 47
Lancaster, PA, 25
Lannum, Joseph, 64
Lannum, William, 64
Lebanon, TN, 12
Leiper's Fork, TN, 32
Lewis, Joel, 60, 105, 107
Lewis, W.B., 49

INDEX

Library of Congress, 49
Lincoln, General Benjamin, 33
Lincoln County, NC, 43, 45
Lincoln County, TN, 33
Lindsay family, 47
Locke, William, 103
Louisa County, VA, 27
Louisiana, State of, 112
Louisiana Territory, 112

M

Mackaness, Perygrine Jr., 42
Mackness' Company, Captain, 43
Mackness, Perrygreen Jr., 44
Magness family, 3, 7, 47, 119
Magness, Arabella (Twitty), 45
Magness, Benjamin, 46
Magness, David, 3, 8, 9, 10, 11, 14, 19, 47, 50, 51, 53, 54, 55, 56, 57, 58, 59, 60, 61, 62, 64, 65, 68, 69, 70, 71, 81, 96, 97, 98, 99, 103, 104, 107, 108, 109, 110, 112, 114, 115, 116, 117, 118
Magness, George, 45
Magness, James, 44, 118
Magness, John, 47, 118
Magness, Jonathan, 4, 8, 9, 10, 12, 14, 41, 42, 44, 45, 46, 47, 50, 51, 52, 53, 54, 56, 57, 58, 59, 61, 62, 64, 70, 71, 78, 80, 82, 86, 89, 94, 100, 101, 102, 103, 104, 105, 106, 108, 109, 110, 111, 113, 114, 115, 116, 117, 118
Magness, Joseph, 45, 46
Magness, Mary (wife of Peregrine Magness Jr.), 42
Magness, Mary (wife of Peregrine Magness Sr.), 42
Magness, Mary Ann, 118
Magness, Morgan, 46, 112, 118
Magness, Peregrine, 50
Magness, Peregrine Jr., 41, 42, 43, 44, 45, 46
Magness, Perigrine Sr., 41, 42
Magness, Peregrine III, 44
Magness, Perry, 14
Magness, Perrygreen, 4, 8, 9, 10, 14, 45, 47, 50, 54, 57, 58, 60, 68, 84, 99, 101, 102, 104, 105, 106, 107, 112, 118
Magness, Robert, 46, 118
Magness, Samuel, 42, 118
Magness, William, 44, 46, 118
Magness, Zachariah, 45
Manley, Caleb, 50
Marshall, John, 25, 26
Marshall, William, 106
Maury County, TN, 33
Mawgridge's case, 77, 78
Mecklenburg County, NC, 43
Memphis, TN, 27, 28
Miles, Thomas, 108
Missouri Inquirer (St. Louis), 35
Missouri Territory, 112, 118
Mitchell, Mark, 106
Mitchell, Thomas, 102, 107
Mitchell, William, 102
Montgomery, Matthew S., 61, 62, 87, 101, 102, 106, 107
Morley case, 76
Morret, James, 108
Muscle Shoals, AL, 51, 58, 59, 82, 86

Mc

McBride, Hugh, 103
McCormick, Mr., 71
McCrory, John, 102
McCulloch, Alex, 64
McCutchen, Samuel, 50
McKellar, Sen. Kenneth D., 24
McLeland, Robert, 50

McLemore, Robert, 106
McNairy, Nathaniel A., 11f
McPeak, John, 105, 107
McQuiston, James, 101, 103, 105, 107

N

Nall, Nicholas, 62, 101, 105
Nally, Major, 64
Nash, William, 106, 107
Nashville Bar Association, 23, 24
Nashville Committee, 30
Nashville Constitutional Advocate, 26
Nashville Jail, 111
Nashville, TN, 26, 28, 30, 32, 34, 37
Natchez, MS, 34
Naylor, George, 42
Neilson, Charles B., 64
New Orleans, LA, 117
Newport, RI, 40
Newsom, Harman, 63, 101
Newsom, Lewis (Old Newsom,)55, 62, 63, 87, 101, 105, 107
Newsom's Tavern (also known as William Newsom's house), 51, 54, 56, 57, 60, 62, 63, 68, 82, 84, 104
Newsom, William, 54, 101, 103, 105, 107
Nolen, William, 108
North Carolina, University of, 32
Null, Nicholas, 107

O

Old, Thomas, 108
Old Times in Tennessee, 19
Oneby case, 95, 96, 97
Orange County, NC, 30
Orleans Territory, 112
Oregon Territory, 36

Overton, John, 11, 12, 14, 15, 27, 28, 29, 30, 67, 74, 75, 76, 98

P

Papers of Andrew Jackson, The, 23
Parks, Reuben, 50
Part of Stoke, 42
Parton, James, 48, 53
Patterson, Andrew, 103
Peacock, William, 103
Peak, John M., 64
Pennsylvania, University of, 25
Perryman, John, 101
Pettway, Hinchey, 111, 118
Phelan, James, 109
Philadelphia, PA, 25
Phillips, 23
Phillips, Joseph, 12, 68, 91, 92, 93, 94, 96, 97
Pitts, Judge John A., 23
Ploughboy (racehorse), 7
Pony Express, 36
Prince George's County, MD, 41, 42
Princeton College, 37
Puckett, Richard, 50

R

Ranier, John, 47
Rawlings, Mr., 12
Reeves, Jordan (aka Jordan Reaves; Jordin Reaves), 23, 47, 54, 56, 61, 69, 70, 71, 72, 102, 103, 104, 105, 107, 118
Reeves, Mary, 118
Reeves, Peter, 50
Reid, John, 3, 23, 49, 55, 65, 67, 72, 74, 81, 98
Revolutionary War, 28, 44
Rice, Elijah, 28
Richmond, VA, 25
Ridley, Thomas, 50

INDEX

Riggs, J., 52, 54
Riggs, Mr., 52, 53, 80
Roberts, John, 106
Robertson, James, 12
Rogers, William, 55, 101, 105, 107
Roosevelt, Theodore, 32
Roundtree, Andrew, 106
Rutherford County, NC, 43, 44, 45, 46
Rutherford County, TN, 33

S

Saddler, John, 61
Scruggs, Dick, 61
Second Regiment of Tennessee Volunteers, 34
Second Seminole War, 39
Selfridge, Trial of, 78
Seminoles (Native American tribe), 39
Sevier, John "Nolichucky Jack," 6
Sharpes' home, 62
Shelbyville, TN, 3, 9, 51, 53, 59, 82, 84, 91, 103
Simpson, Archibald, 61, 101, 107
Simpson, William, 101, 107
Sims, William, 43
St. Louis, MO, 35
Stones River, TN, 47
Stuart, Thomas (Bedford Co. Circuit Judge), 10, 14, 50, 107
Stuart's Creek (Wilson County, Tennessee), 47
Stubblefield, Jeanette, 46
Superior Court of North Carolina, 20
Superior Court of Tennessee, 11
Supreme Court of Tennessee, 26, 30

T

Tarkinton, Jessee, 106
Tennessee General Assembly, 112, 116, 117
Tennessee House of Representatives, 18
Tennessee Legislature, 18
Tennessee Militia, 5
Tennessee Superior Court, 11, 28
Tennessee Supreme Court, 6, 20
Tennessee Supreme Court of Errors and Appeals, 28
Terry, Keeble, 103
Thirteenth Congress, 18
Thirty-third Congress, 36
Thomson, Col., 44
Thomson's Regiment of South Carolina Rangers, 44
Traveller's Rest, 30
Treasury Department (U.S), 38
Trenton, NJ, 25
Truxton (racehorse), 7
Tune, William, 12, 57, 58, 60, 61, 84, 85, 106
Twelfth Congress, 18
Tyler, John, 40
Tyron Committee of Safety (North Carolina), 43
Tyron County, NC, 43, 44
Tyron County Court (North Carolina), 43
Tyron Militia (North Carolina), 44
Tyron Regiment of Militia (Graham's), 44
Tyron Resolves (North Carolina), 43, 44

U

University of North Carolina, 32
University of Pennsylvania, 25

U.S. House of Representatives, 6, 35, 36
U.S. Senate, 6, 12f, 18, 25, 26, 35, 36
U.S. Treasury Department 38
U.S. War Department, 39

V

Van Buren, Martin, 18, 38, 39
Virginia House of Burgesses, 42

W

Wade, Edward, 12
Walker, James, 103
Walker, Thomas, 50
War Department (U.S.), 34
War of 1812, 117
Ward, Edward, 56, 64, 106, 107
Warren County, KY, 46
Washington, George, 28, 42
Washington, D.C., 26, 34
Watson, Thomas E., 34, 35
Webb, Thomas, 42
West, Col. John, 42
White, Jessee, 108
White River (Missouri Territory), 118
Whiteside, Jenkin, 11, 15, 23, 24, 25, 26, 27, 33, 57, 67, 70, 74, 91, 98
Williams, Claiborne, 105, 107
Williams, Emma Inman, 23
Williams, G., Esq., 64
Williams, Isaac "Ike," 54, 56, 63, 101, 105, 107
Williams, Nat., 60
Williamson County, TN, 11, 14, 37, 50, 99, 102, 103, 105, 108, 110, 113, 115
Williamson, Judge Nathaniel, 104, 108, 110
Williamson, Thomas, JP, 114, 116
Wills, James, 105
Wilson County, TN, 47, 71
Wilson, James A., 103
Winchester, Gen. James, 28
Woodford County, KY, 45
Wright, Mr., 58
Wytheville, VA, 26

About the Author

JACK MACGREGOR (MAC) CAMPBELL, is a native of Harrison, Arkansas. He holds degrees in agricultural economics and law from the University of Arkansas and a Master of Laws in taxation from Georgetown University. In his career, he has served as Legislative Assistant and Tax Counsel to U.S. Senator Blanche L. Lincoln of Arkansas, Legislative Director for U.S. Senator Maria E. Cantwell of Washington State, and as the Deputy Staff Director and General Counsel of the U.S. Senate Finance Committee under Chairman Max Baucus of Montana. He was an Assistant U.S. Trade Representative in the Administration of President Barack Obama. Currently, he is Senior Vice-President of the Lincoln Policy Group, a public policy consulting and lobbying firm. He lives in Washington, DC with his wife Katie and their dog Archie.

www.ingramcontent.com/pod-product-compliance
Lightning Source LLC
Chambersburg PA
CBHW071736080526
44588CB00013B/2052